THE BEGINNER'S GUIDE TO *Gluten-Free* VEGAN BAKING

60 Easy Plant-Based Desserts for Any Occasion

Gina Fontana, creator of Healthy Little Vittles

PAGE STREET
PUBLISHING CO.

Contents

INTRODUCTION

Revamping your diet and lifestyle can be hard and stressful. I get it. When I first started my journey nearly seven years ago, I felt lost, hopeless, frustrated and very sad that I had to give up many of my favorite foods. I found myself wallowing in self-pity, wishing I could eat this or that, sneaking foods that I knew would make me feel ill, only to be sent on a downward spiral. There just came a day when I was just so sick of being sick, and I knew I had to take control of it.

What needed to change first? I needed to *change my mind-set.* I began researching and learning and practicing in the kitchen. I spent more time reading labels at the grocery store, and I started including more fresh, whole foods in my diet as opposed to processed stuff that comes in boxes. Little by little, I started to crowd out the "bad" stuff and replace what I thought were my favorite foods with healthier alternatives that soon became the new foundation of my diet. And when I say "diet," I don't mean the kind you try and seemingly fail at—diets don't work, friends. It's really all about lifestyle changes, both big and small, that enhance our quality of life so that we can be the best versions of ourselves and carry out the tasks that God created us for.

Savory foods were pretty easy. I got the hang of that relatively quickly. However, gluten-free, vegan baking is not only challenging at times, but it also might not compare to the way we used to enjoy our desserts. But because going gluten-free and vegan wasn't a "choice" for me, rather it was essential for my health, that held me accountable and kept pushing me forward. Today, I can say that I feel confident in my gluten-free, vegan dessert-making, and I find these recipes to be quite delicious and comparable to the "real" versions. I am just so grateful that there are other ways to indulge in my favorite sweet treats, and I am so incredibly excited to share these dessert recipes with you!

What have I learned most? If we *keep an open mind,* we keep experimenting. When we *express gratitude* for new ways of enjoying our faves, then anything baked with that kind of outlook will turn out great, even if it does take a few tries. Where there's a will, there's a way—and my carb-craving, sugar-loving sweet tooth wasn't ready to ditch desserts altogether, so here we are!

I'm extremely grateful for my health and for this journey it has led me on, and I hope that you will love these recipes as much as my family and I do. If you make any of them, please don't forget to leave a comment on my blog, Healthy Little Vittles, or tag me on Instagram or Facebook, @HealthyLittleVittles. I truly do desire to help other people find ways of enjoying all kinds of culinary creations. I want to inspire people to indulge in a way that doesn't force the choice of their happiness over their health and vice versa, and to mindfully acknowledge the need to pursue food freedom—because your mental health matters too. We just have to find a way to indulge smarter . . . and differently, and we can certainly do that together!

You are not alone, my friend. As food allergies and sensitivities are on the rise, I wanted to create a cookbook that allows families and friends to still come together and enjoy dessert, because I know all too well how it feels to be "left out," wishing you could have a slice of that perfect birthday cake. Well now you can have your cake and eat it too! Whether you have food allergies yourself, want to thoughtfully include someone who does or simply seek healthier dessert alternatives, this is the book for you. I hope the way this book is organized by problem-solving scenarios will guide you toward success in your gluten-free, vegan baking excursions, as I have experienced all of these baking scenarios myself. My intention is that this book will prove to be one that gets you started, keeps you going and brings you happiness and comfort along the way.

Many Healthy Blessings,
xoxo Gina

Gluten-Free
FLOUR 101

Baking can be a challenging task, and if I'm being 100 percent honest, I was not necessarily born to be a baker. It's not something that comes easily to me. You'd think because I'm a very precise, detail-oriented person that baking would be my forte, but I'm more of a throw-in-some-of-this, add-a-dash-of-that-and-see-what-happens kinda chef. Cut gluten out of the mix, quite literally, and you can imagine how intimidated I was when it came to making sweet treats for my blog, Healthy Little Vittles. I dared to take it a step further and added the vegan component to baking, and then there was a whole new mountain to climb. I've certainly had my fair share (maybe more than fair) of failed recipes, but I kept practicing and experimenting with different ingredients until I finally felt like I cracked the code.

A BRIEF INTRODUCTION TO GLUTEN-FREE FLOUR

Over the last five years or so, gluten-free flour has come a very long way. When I first started out on my journey, the pickings were slim; they were hard to find, and they weren't all that great. I thought bakery items as I knew them were gone. Fast-forward to 2021. With the baking industry making some major strides (and me practicing and practicing), I'm very happy to report that baked desserts are back on the table! I am so grateful for the different choices now! Yay! And the truth is, nothing will ever live up to the fluffy, tender texture that gluten-filled flours provide. After all, that's gluten's number one job, but the good news is (and remember it's partly your mind-set) you can come pretty darn close and still satisfy your dessert craving with gluten-free, vegan alternatives that don't leave you feeling bloated, sluggish and downright awful. That being said, I've discovered that all gluten-free flours are not equal. So, I hope to shed some light and offer my advice on what I have found to be the recipe for success in your baking excursions.

Gluten-Free All-Purpose 1:1 Baking Flour

Unlike all-purpose flour made from wheat, gluten-free all-purpose flour is made with a combination of different wheat-free flours. Some of the most popular gluten-free flours are made from rice, oat, almond, sorghum, potato, arrowroot, buckwheat, teff, amaranth, corn, chickpea, coconut, tapioca, cassava and more! I like to use a 1:1 baking flour that is a mixture of white rice, brown rice, sorghum and potato flours and tapioca starch. The proportion of each flour in the mix absolutely matters, so when I find a flour that I like, I tend to stick to it.

GRAIN-FREE FLOUR

Try a grain-free flour! Currently some of my favorite flours to use for baking also happen to be grain-free. Cassava flour, almond flour, coconut flour, sweet potato flour and banana flour are my favorites! Because a lot of the dessert recipes in this book use these popular flours, let's dive a little deeper into them.

Cassava Flour

Made from the root of a cassava plant (also known as yuca), cassava flour has a texture that's a bit starchy, similar to a yam or potato. I find the light and fine texture to be wonderful in my baked goods. In fact, cassava flour, out of all the gluten-free flour options, is considered to be the most comparable to regular all-purpose flour! I find that it's not quite as dense as some of the other gluten-free flours either, so it really allows for lighter baked goods. Not all cassava flour brands are equal; some leave your batter a puddly mess, so if that happens, try a different brand. I've listed two brands of cassava flour that I use the most in the Special Ingredients & Favorite Brands section (page 160).

Almond Flour

If you don't have a nut sensitivity or allergy, almond flour is an amazing option. My favorite way to enjoy almond flour is in no-bake or raw desserts, like in my raw Edible Chocolate Chip Cookie Dough recipe (page 124). Aside from almonds delivering massive amounts of nutrients, they are also loaded with antioxidants. So you can totally call my almond flour dessert recipes "healthy." *Wink*.

Coconut Flour

Although coconut flour is a bit more difficult to bake with compared to other flours—because it absorbs a lot of moisture and can sometimes make baked goods dry and crumbly—it is still a viable option. I find that I like to combine the coconut flour with other flours, such as cassava, oat or banana flour. However, it is safe to eat raw, which makes it a great candidate for raw recipes. With a mild taste—as in not having an intense coconut flavor (for all the non-coconut lovers out there), it blends well with the other ingredients in the recipe while offering a similar traditional flour texture. I love to use coconut flour in crumb bar, cupcake and crust recipes.

Sweet Potato Flour

You guessed it—sweet potato flour is made from sweet potatoes! Pretty neat, huh? It's one of my newest discoveries. Only a few select brands are producing it, so it could be a little difficult to find. However, it's a great grain-free option. I happen to love sweet potatoes (they might be my favorite food!), so I find the flour to be delicious in my dessert recipes because it offers just a tad of sweetness while helping to maintain a little bit of moisture when replacing or enhancing other flours in baked goods. You can also use it in pancakes or waffles. Yum!

Banana Flour

Banana flour?! What?! Oh, it exists, my friend, and it's actually one of my favorite flours! It is definitely becoming more popular. It doesn't get nearly the amount of praise it should, but I love using banana flour. Banana flour is made by peeling, chopping, drying and grinding green bananas into a fine flour. Contrary to what you might think, banana flour has a fairly mild banana flavor, so it's not overpowering in recipes. If you're unable to find banana flour locally, you may be able to do this at home by dehydrating or baking the bananas (sliced), then grinding them into flour. I buy mine online and am sure to keep it on hand at all times for when my sweet tooth hits.

While there are lots of recipes from other chapters that involve the use of gluten-free flours, I chose these specific recipes for this chapter because I feel as though these are the hardest to really nail when subbing all-purpose flour with gluten-free flour, and they are the recipes that I found to be the most challenging. Sometimes gluten-free baking is a science of figuring out the perfect combination of flours or the exact right amount to substitute for a recipe. I have gone through a lot of trial and error to discover the perfect ratios in the following desserts.

TAHINI CHOCOLATE CHIP SKILLET COOKIE

No plates are needed for this fun dessert, just grab a spoon and dig right in! This easy chocolate chip skillet cookie is made with banana flour, making this recipe not only gluten-free and vegan, but also grain-free and nut-free. Enjoy with a scoop or two of my No-Churn Vanilla Ice Cream (page 153) on top for ooey, gooey, melty perfection!

Preheat the oven to 350°F (175°C). Spray or grease a 10-inch (25-cm) oven-safe skillet with coconut oil or butter. In a large bowl, whisk together the banana flour, baking powder and salt and set aside. In another large bowl, beat together the butter and vanilla until creamy, then add the sugar, pumpkin puree and tahini and beat until combined. Gradually add the flour mixture to the wet mixture, beating on low until a cookie dough forms, adding 1 tablespoon (15 ml) of plant milk at a time if needed. Your batter should be sticky, not dry and crumbly. Turn the beater off and fold in the chocolate chips.

Press the cookie dough into the prepared skillet using a rubber spatula or your fingers and bake for 15 to 18 minutes. Let it cool in the skillet for about 10 minutes before serving. Top with No-Churn Vanilla Ice Cream, if desired.

YIELD: *6 servings*

SKILLET COOKIE

2 cups (240 g) banana flour

1½ tsp (7 g) baking powder

¼ tsp salt

¼ cup (54 g) vegan butter, softened

1 tsp pure vanilla extract

½ cup (65 g) coconut or date sugar

¾ cup (184 g) pure pumpkin puree

½ cup (120 g) tahini

2 to 4 tbsp (30 to 60 ml) plant milk, as needed

1 cup (168 g) dark chocolate chips

TOPPING

No-Churn Vanilla Ice Cream (page 153; optional)

GRAIN-FREE VANILLA CUPCAKES WITH STRAWBERRY FROSTING

Nothing beats a classic vanilla cupcake stacked with frosting. To make these cupcakes even better, say hello to real pink strawberry frosting! Not only are these beauties simple to make, but they are also grain-free, making them a top candidate for your next birthday party!

To start the strawberry frosting, add the strawberries and maple syrup to a small saucepan and heat the berries over medium-high heat until they reduce and you're left with a jam-like mixture, stirring occasionally so it doesn't stick to the bottom. This should take 15 to 20 minutes. Smash any large strawberry chunks with a fork. Remove from the heat and transfer to the fridge to cool while you make the cupcakes.

To start the cupcakes, in a glass bowl or measuring cup, whisk together the milk, vinegar, vanilla, maple syrup and oil and let it sit for about 10 minutes.

Preheat the oven to 350°F (175°C). In a large bowl, whisk together the cassava flour, almond flour, coconut flour, salt, baking soda, baking powder and cinnamon, then add the wet ingredients and stir just enough to form a batter.

Line a cupcake pan, then fill each liner about two-thirds full with batter. Bake for 15 minutes, or until the cupcakes have risen and a toothpick inserted into the center of a cupcake comes out clean. Let the cupcakes cool in the cupcake pan for about 10 minutes, then transfer to a cooling rack to cool completely before frosting.

To finish the strawberry frosting, cream together the butter, shortening and vanilla with an electric mixer until smooth and creamy. Add the strawberry flavoring mixture and whip until incorporated, then add the confectioners' sugar, a little bit at a time. Transfer the frosting to a piping bag and frost the cupcakes after they've cooled completely. Store any leftover cupcakes uncovered on your counter for 1 day, then transfer to an airtight container and store in the fridge for up to 3 days.

YIELD: *8–9 cupcakes*

STRAWBERRY FROSTING

1 cup (166 g) strawberries, diced

1 tbsp (15 ml) maple syrup

½ cup (108 g) vegan butter

½ cup (103 g) vegan shortening

1 tsp pure vanilla extract

4 cups (480 g) confectioners' sugar

CUPCAKES

⅔ cup plus ½ cup (280 ml) almond milk

2 tsp (10 ml) apple cider vinegar

1 tsp pure vanilla extract

½ cup (120 ml) maple syrup

¼ cup (60 ml) avocado oil

½ cup (61 g) cassava flour

½ cup (48 g) almond flour

½ cup (56 g) coconut flour

¼ tsp salt

½ tsp baking soda

1 tsp baking powder

Pinch of cinnamon

NOTE: *If the frosting is too runny, you can add more confectioners' sugar.*

BANANA CAKE

Think banana bread but in cake form frosted with vegan cream cheese icing. If you're a banana lover, you're going to really love this banana cake. I'm using one of my favorite flours in this banana cake to make this recipe extra special. The banana flour not only enhances the banana flavor, but it makes this recipe grain-free. And shoot, since it's pretty much banana bread, you go ahead and have yourself a slice for breakfast too! *Wink.*

Preheat the oven to 350°F (175°C). To make flax eggs, combine the flaxseed meal and water in a small bowl and set it aside for about 5 minutes to "gel up." In a large bowl, whisk together the flour, tapioca starch, baking soda, baking powder, cinnamon and salt. In a separate bowl, combine the bananas, milk, vanilla, maple syrup, nut or seed butter and prepared flax eggs. Pour the wet ingredients into the dry and stir to combine. Don't overmix. Pour the batter into a greased 7 x 11–inch (18 x 28–cm) cake pan and bake for 35 to 45 minutes, until a toothpick inserted into the center comes out clean and the top of the cake is nice and golden.

To make the cream cheese icing, beat the butter and cream cheese together until smooth, then add the sugar a little bit at a time until the frosting forms. Allow the banana cake to cool completely before frosting. Store covered on your counter for up to 3 days.

NOTE: *You may also use a 9 x 13–inch (23 x 33–cm) cake pan. The cake will just be thinner. If you do use a 9 x 13–inch (23 x 33–cm) cake pan, check the cake at 25 to 30 minutes to see if the toothpick comes out clean.*

YIELD: *9–12 servings*

BANANA CAKE

4 tbsp (28 g) flaxseed meal

⅔ cup (160 ml) water

2 cups (240 g) banana flour

1 cup (130 g) tapioca starch

2 tsp (9 g) baking soda

2 tsp (9 g) baking powder

1 tsp cinnamon

½ tsp salt

3 large bananas, ripe and smashed with a fork

1 cup (240 ml) plant milk

1 tsp pure vanilla extract

1 cup (240 ml) maple syrup

½ cup (129 g) peanut butter or sunflower seed butter, or other preferred nut butter

CREAM CHEESE ICING

½ cup (108 g) vegan butter, softened

½ cup (120 g) vegan cream cheese

2 cups (240 g) confectioners' sugar

GINGER PEACH GALETTES

A ginger-infused, graham-style mini pie crust gets folded over allspice and cinnamon peaches and garnished with sliced almonds. You can drizzle these galettes with maple or agave syrup to keep it naturally sweetened and top with a scoop of dairy-free vanilla ice cream for the most delicious gluten-free vegan dessert!

Preheat your oven to 400°F (205°C). In a food processor, process the granola, baking soda, cinnamon, ginger, salt and flour. Pour the mixture into a bowl and add the almond butter, maple syrup and vanilla and stir until a dough forms. Add a little more flour if it's too sticky. Once your dough is formed, place it onto your floured countertop or a floured piece of parchment paper.

Divide the dough in half. Using an oiled rolling pin and your hands, roll out each half into 7-inch (18-cm) circles on the floured piece of parchment paper. If the dough breaks apart when rolling, put it back in the bowl and add water, 1 tablespoon (15 ml) at a time. Once both of the crusts are rolled out, carefully move the parchment paper onto a baking sheet.

To make the filling, add the peaches to a separate bowl. Add the tapioca starch or arrowroot powder, allspice, cinnamon and sugar and stir gently to combine. Moving clockwise, layer the peach slices in a fanlike pattern in the center of both galettes, leaving about a 1-inch (2.5-cm) border to fold the crust over the ends of the peaches. Fold the dough over the ends of the peaches using a knife to help you fold the dough smoothly. If it breaks, just pinch the dough back together with your fingers. Continue in either a clockwise or counterclockwise pattern until all the dough is folded over. Repeat with the other galette.

Next, spray the peaches with coconut oil, brush some plant milk over the crust and garnish with sliced almonds. Sprinkle the crust and peaches with more cinnamon, if desired, and bake for 40 minutes. Serve with dairy-free vanilla ice cream and maple or agave syrup, if desired.

YIELD: *2 galettes*

GINGER GRAHAM-STYLE CRUST

2 cups (206 g) gluten-free granola

1 tsp baking soda

½ tsp cinnamon

1 tsp ground ginger

Pinch of salt

½ cup (61 g) cassava flour, plus more if needed

½ cup (125 g) almond butter

½ cup (120 ml) maple syrup

1 tsp pure vanilla extract

FILLING

2 cups (570 g) peaches, peeled and sliced (fresh or canned)

½ tbsp (4 g) tapioca starch or arrowroot powder

⅛ tsp allspice

⅛ tsp cinnamon

2 tbsp (16 g) coconut or date sugar

TOPPING

Plant milk

Sliced almonds

Cinnamon (optional)

Dairy-free vanilla ice cream (optional)

Maple or agave syrup (optional)

APPLE BUTTER
WHOOPIE PIES

These gluten-free, vegan mini whoopie pies are so pillowy soft, and they incorporate apple butter mixed right into the cookie batter to keep them moist. They are then stuffed with a bourbon-infused cinnamon buttercream frosting and more apple butter for the perfect cookie treat. The bourbon is optional—even if you don't include it, I think you're going to love these little gems!

Preheat the oven to 375°F (190°C). Lay out two macaron baking mats onto baking sheets.

Make your flax eggs by combining the flaxseed meal and water in a small bowl and letting it sit for a few minutes until it "gels up."

To make the cookies, in a large bowl, beat the butter, nut or seed butter, vanilla and sugar with an electric mixer on medium speed, scraping the bowl occasionally, until well blended. Beat in the apple butter and flax eggs until well mixed.

On low speed, beat in the flour, baking soda, baking powder, cinnamon, allspice and salt.

Using macaron baking mats makes piping the cookies easier and more uniform, but if you're not using macaron baking mats, just be sure to pipe 1½-inch (4-cm) circles of batter per cookie on a parchment paper–lined baking sheet, leaving ¾ inch (2 cm) of space between each.

Fill a pastry bag fitted with a round piping tip, or a gallon plastic bag with one tip cut off, with the dough and pipe the cookie dough to fill the outer circle. You don't want the piped cookie batter to be too thin, so I like to keep the piping tip in the middle and make tiny movements while piping the batter until the circle is full. Once all the batter is piped onto the mat-lined baking sheets, bake them for 10 minutes and cool them on the mats for 15 to 20 minutes before filling with the frosting.

(continued)

APPLE BUTTER COOKIES

2 tbsp (14 g) flaxseed meal

5 tbsp (75 ml) water

½ cup (108 g) vegan butter, softened

¼ cup (63 g) nut or seed butter (like cashew, almond or sunflower seed butter, see Note)

1 tsp pure vanilla extract

1 cup (130 g) coconut sugar

½ cup (136 g) apple butter

2 cups (296 g) gluten-free all-purpose flour (preferably 1:1 baking flour)

1 tsp baking soda

1 tsp baking powder

½ tsp cinnamon

¼ tsp allspice

Pinch of salt

APPLE BUTTER
WHOOPIE PIES (CONT.)

To make the frosting, in a stand mixer, cream the butter, bourbon (if using), cinnamon and vanilla on medium speed. Slowly add in the confectioners' sugar and keep blending until it thickens.

To assemble the whoopie pies, when the cookies are cool, pipe the bottom of one cookie with the buttercream frosting, leaving a small border around the edge. Spread some apple butter on the other cookie, then place that cookie on top of the buttercream to make a sandwich. Store in an airtight container in the fridge for up to 3 days. You can freeze them too!

NOTE: *If you use sunflower seed butter, your cookies may turn green as they cool. This completely harmless phenomenon happens because the chlorophyll in the sunflower seeds reacts with the baking soda and baking powder when baked, causing the green color.*

BOURBON CINNAMON BUTTERCREAM FROSTING

1 cup (215 g) vegan butter

2 tsp (10 ml) bourbon (optional)

¼ tsp cinnamon

1 tsp pure vanilla extract

3½ cups (420 g) confectioners' sugar

FILLING

2 to 4 tbsp (34 to 68 g) apple butter

MADE-FROM-SCRATCH CHERRY PIE

The classic and infinitely popular cherry pie gets a gluten-free, vegan, not-from-a-can makeover! This cherry pie is also made with less and natural sugar, allowing the cherries to really shine. You can make this pie from scratch year-round by using fresh pitted cherries or frozen cherries.

Preheat the oven to 400°F (205°C). Grease a 9-inch (23-cm) pie plate with vegan butter or spray coconut oil.

In a large bowl, whisk together the flours, salt and sugar (if using). Next, add both the oil and butter and knead the dough with your hands or a pastry cutter. Add the water and continue to knead until your pie dough can roll into a ball.

Divide the dough in half and set aside half of the dough to place over the cherry filling. Press the other half of the dough into the sides of the greased pie plate first, then into the bottom of the pie plate and set aside.

NOTE: *Because gluten-free dough isn't as bendable and elastic as regular pie dough, you have to be more careful. If you get cracks, just squeeze them back together with your fingers. Be extra careful not to press too hard with the top crust to expose the cherry pie filling.*

(continued)

YIELD: *6–8 servings*

PIE CRUST

4 cups (592 g) gluten-free baking flour

1 cup (112 g) coconut flour

2 tsp (12 g) salt

4 tbsp (32 g) coconut or date sugar (optional)

⅔ cup (147 g) coconut oil, softened but not completely melted

1 cup (215 g) vegan butter

12 to 14 tbsp (180 to 210 ml) water, ice cold

To make the filling, place the cherries in a medium saucepan over medium heat until they start to simmer and the juices release. Add the coconut or date sugar and stir the cherries continuously to prevent burning. Next, combine the tapioca starch and lemon juice in a small bowl and stir until the starch is dissolved. Pour the mixture into the saucepan with the cherries, add the vanilla and salt and stir. Continue to heat the mixture, stirring constantly, until the mixture starts to thicken, about 2 minutes. Pour the cherry pie filling into your prepared crust, then set aside.

Set a piece of wax paper onto your counter; it should be a bit larger than your pie plate. Carefully roll out the second pie crust onto the wax paper. Very carefully, flip the dough over top of the cherry filling and ruffle the edges to match the bottom crust. Carefully make an X in the middle of the pie to allow it to vent.

Using a pastry brush (or a clean paintbrush), brush milk over top of the crust and, if using, sprinkle sparkling sugar over the top.

Place the pie into the oven and bake for 20 minutes at 400°F (205°C). Reduce the heat to 375°F (190°C) and bake for another 30 minutes. Remove from the oven and let it cool.

CHERRY PIE FILLING

30 oz (850 g) pitted cherries, frozen or fresh (if using frozen, thaw before use)

½ cup (65 g) coconut or date sugar

¼ cup (33 g) tapioca starch

2 tbsp (30 ml) lemon juice

1 tsp pure vanilla extract

Pinch of salt

TOPPING

Plant milk

Sparkling sugar (optional)

BERRY CRUMB BARS

These crumb bars are a blend of raspberries, blackberries and blueberries stuffed between two layers of gluten-free, grain-free crumble and make for the perfect simple berry dessert. I first developed berry crumb bars with my foodie friend Natalie from Feasting on Fruit and decided to adapt them to make them grain-free! You can easily just use one type of berry or switch out the berries for any combination you'd like. Also, frozen berries can be used in place of fresh berries. The crust is tenacious enough to hold up as the bottom layer, yet crumbly enough be the perfect streusel-esque topping. It's a one-and-done type of crust situation, so this recipe is already a winner. Add the delicious berry layer and this recipe could easily become one of your favorite year-round sweet treats!

Preheat the oven to 350°F (175°C). Line an 8 x 8–inch (20 x 20–cm) baking pan with parchment paper. In a medium-large saucepan, add the berries, sugar, tapioca starch or arrowroot powder and lemon juice and heat over medium heat until the berries start to reduce and the filling thickens. Be sure to stir frequently to avoid sticking to the bottom of the pan.

To make the crust, in a large bowl, whisk together the flours, sugar, baking soda, cinnamon and salt. Add the oil, nut or seed butter, vanilla and lemon juice to a glass measuring cup and melt it in the microwave for 30 to 45 seconds. Once it is melted, stir to combine. Add the melted mixture to the dry crust ingredients and stir to combine, until a crumble-like texture forms.

Press half of the crumble mixture into the parchment paper–lined baking pan. Pour in the berry filling, then sprinkle the rest of the crumble on top. Bake for 25 to 30 minutes. Allow it to fully cool before slicing. Keep the bars stored in an airtight container in your fridge or freeze some for later!

YIELD: *9–12 bars*

FILLING

4 cups (760 g) berries (may use a mixture of berries)

3 tbsp (24 g) coconut or date sugar

2 tbsp (16 g) tapioca starch or arrowroot powder

1 tbsp (15 ml) lemon juice

CRUST

1 cup (122 g) cassava flour

1 cup (96 g) almond flour

¼ cup (28 g) coconut flour

⅔ cup (87 g) coconut or date sugar

½ tsp baking soda

½ tsp cinnamon

¼ tsp salt

½ cup (110 g) coconut oil

½ cup (126 g) nut or seed butter

1 tsp pure vanilla extract

1 tbsp (15 ml) lemon juice

SALTED PEANUT BUTTER ALMOND FLOUR COOKIES

You can't ever go wrong with a classic cookie recipe, and these peanut butter cookies sure live up to their popular cookie status. Swap out regular flour with almond flour, sweeten them with agave syrup and sprinkle them with sea salt for the perfect salty-sweet, healthier peanut butter cookie that won't disappoint.

Preheat the oven to 325°F (160°C). Line two 9 x 13–inch (23 x 33–cm) baking sheets with parchment paper. In a large bowl, whisk together the flour and baking soda and set aside. In a glass measuring cup or bowl, melt the peanut butter and vegan butter in the microwave for 30 seconds, or until smooth. Add the vanilla and agave syrup to the melted peanut butter mixture and stir to combine.

Pour the melted peanut butter mixture into the bowl with the almond flour and baking soda and stir to create a cookie dough. Using a cookie scoop or a spoon, scoop 2-tablespoon (about 43-g) portions of dough onto the prepared baking sheets, leaving a little space in between the cookies. Using the back of a fork, gently press each cookie down, then turn the fork and press down the other way, making a crisscross pattern. Repeat for all of the cookies and garnish with sea salt. Bake them for 10 to 12 minutes. Let them cool before enjoying.

NOTE: *For peanut-free cookies, simply swap out the peanut butter for sunflower seed butter, almond butter, cashew butter, etc.*

YIELD: *12 cookies*

1½ cups (144 g) almond flour

½ tsp baking soda

½ cup (129 g) unsweetened peanut butter, creamy

¼ cup (54 g) vegan butter

1 tsp pure vanilla extract

4 tbsp (60 ml) agave syrup

Coarse sea salt, for garnishing (large flake if available)

GRAIN-FREE BLACKBERRY LINZER COOKIES

I have always wanted to make Linzer cookies! This was my first attempt at a recipe, and let me tell you, I've been missing out! These cookies are so delicious and perfect for any occasion, but especially for the holidays. The cookie dough is made grain-free with almond and coconut flours and tapioca starch. Sandwiched in between is an easy, homemade blackberry jam for one marvelous-yet-simple cookie recipe!

Line a baking sheet with parchment paper. Preheat the oven to 375°F (190°C). To make the blackberry filling, add the blackberries, lemon juice, maple syrup and tapioca starch or arrowroot powder to a medium saucepan and heat over medium heat until the blackberries start to reduce and the filling thickens, 10 to 15 minutes. Be sure to stir frequently to avoid sticking to the bottom of the pan. While the blackberries are simmering, make the cookies.

In a large bowl, whisk together the flours, tapioca starch, cinnamon, baking powder and salt. Add the maple syrup, oil or butter and vanilla and stir it with a spatula or spoon until a dough forms. Place the dough onto a large piece of parchment paper and then place another piece of parchment paper on top of the dough and roll the dough out to ¼- to ½-inch (6-mm to 1.3-cm) thickness.

Using a round cookie cutter or even a glass, cut rounds from the dough and place half of them onto the prepared baking sheets. Cookie-cut the centers out of the remaining half of the dough rounds and set aside. You want the holes to be large enough to show the blackberry filling, but you still want to have enough cookie dough to ensure the rounds don't fall apart.

Next, place 1 teaspoon of the blackberry mixture in the center of each uncut round, almost to the edges but leaving a border. Place the cookie-cut dough round on top of the filling and gently press the top and bottom rounds together to seal the edges of the dough. Bake for 10 minutes and let them cool before enjoying. Store uncovered on your counter for up to 3 days.

YIELD: *10 cookie sandwiches*

BLACKBERRY FILLING

2 cups (288 g) blackberries, frozen or fresh

½ tbsp (8 ml) lemon juice

2 tbsp (30 ml) maple syrup

1 tbsp (8 g) tapioca starch or arrowroot powder

COOKIES

1 cup (96 g) almond flour

½ cup (56 g) coconut flour

½ cup (65 g) tapioca starch

½ tsp cinnamon

½ tsp baking powder

1 tsp salt

⅓ cup (80 ml) maple syrup

⅓ cup (80 ml) coconut oil or vegan butter, melted

1 tsp pure vanilla extract

Now That's Sweet!
(NATURAL SWEETENERS)

This is totally a personal preference, but you will notice in most of my baking recipes I keep things refined sugar–free. I usually opt for natural sweeteners like maple syrup, agave syrup, date syrup, tapioca syrup, coconut sugar and date sugar. Those are my go-tos, but I will use organic cane and confectioners' sugar on occasion. You can try to replace my suggested natural sweeteners with regular sugar, but I cannot guarantee the same results. My suggestion would be to try using natural sugars and see how you like it—you might be surprised!

I think we all know that *too much* sugar isn't good for us; the "problem" is we love sugar too dang much! Trust me, I'm there with ya. So, here's what I told myself. Instead of making myself feel guilty about eating too much artificial, refined sugar that proved to have no nutritional value at all, I could allow myself to mindfully indulge in the unrefined, natural sugars and when consumed in small amounts, maybe even reap some nutritional benefits (again, when consumed in small amounts). Here are my top six go-to natural sugars, and some potential benefits, other than satisfying your sweet tooth.

Maple Syrup
From the sap of maple trees, maple syrup is probably the most recognized natural sweetener in the group and the one I use most often. Other than for pouring on your pancakes, maple syrup in its purest form can provide small amounts of minerals and antioxidants—again, in *small* amounts. It raises your blood sugar slower than table sugar does, so I find it to be a better option to avoid that sugar-high feeling.

Agave Syrup
Agave syrup comes from the sap of a blue agave plant, the same plant that sources tequila! Agave syrup is more processed than maple syrup and it is sweeter, so you don't need to use as much. I like agave syrup because it has a lower glycemic index value (how fast it makes your blood sugar rise); it actually has the lowest GI value out of table sugar, honey and maple syrup!

Date Syrup

Syrup that comes from dates is another up-and-coming natural sweetener. It has more than twice the potassium, calcium and magnesium levels of maple syrup or honey, with up to ten times the antioxidants, making it a front-runner! I also really love the robust, rich flavor it gives my baked goods. It's the least processed as well, keeping most of the nutrients in the syrup. This might be your best option, so I definitely suggest giving it a try. The only downside is that date syrup is very dark and will darken your batter, so just keep that in mind when selecting this form of natural sweetener.

Tapioca Syrup

Derived from the cassava root (a favorite flour of mine too, if you remember!), tapioca syrup can also be used as a sugar replacement, but it's very thick and relatively flavorless, so I use it more commonly as a corn syrup replacement. The downside is that it's a bit hard to find; you'll probably have to order it online.

Coconut Sugar

From the palm of a coconut (not the coconut itself), coconut sugar is made from boiled sap that is dehydrated to create a sugar; this is one of the more popular cane sugar replacements out there. Coconut sugar is a great low-fructose option as well, and it has a low glycemic index value, which makes it a great alternative. Like the others, it does contain some nutrients as well. Coconut sugar is a great brown sugar replacement and can offer a slight hint of a caramel flavoring. It will turn your desserts more brown, as it's not processed to be white like table sugar, so keep that in mind.

Date Sugar

Date sugar is made from ground and dehydrated dates. This one is a great brown sugar replacement also. Date sugar is a bit harder to find than coconut sugar, but it doesn't have that mild underlying coconut flavor like coconut sugar does. So if you're not a fan of coconut, date sugar may be a great option for you. Date sugar, like the others, has some great vitamins and minerals and is also high in fiber. Date sugar doesn't dissolve like regular sugar does, so it's best used in baking, not in beverages.

When natural sweeteners are used in combination with foods that are sweet by nature, such as fruit or coconut, you'll find that the added cane sugar isn't even really missed.

BAKED CHOCOLATE GANACHE CHEESECAKE

Cheesecake is one of my all-time favorite desserts. I would often ask for cheesecake in place of regular cake for my birthday and loved my grandmother's recipe so much. This baked chocolate ganache cheesecake is adapted from her recipe to be made gluten-free and vegan, and it doesn't use any replacement cream cheese products. I use a combination of cashews, flax eggs and coconut cream to make the perfect cheesecake texture that you won't believe is vegan, then I top it with a lush layer of my chocolate ganache for an unbelievably drool-worthy dessert.

Preheat the oven to 325°F (160°C). Grease a 9-inch (23-cm) springform pan. Add the cashews to a medium saucepan and cover with water. Boil them for 15 minutes. In the meantime, to make flax eggs, in a small bowl combine the flaxseed meal and water and set it aside.

Next, make the crust by combining the oats, flour, cocoa powder, sugar, cinnamon and salt in a food processor or blender and pulse to combine. Add the oil and vanilla and pulse until a sticky dough forms. Press the dough into the bottom of the prepared springform pan.

Drain and rinse the cashews. In the food processor or blender, add the butter, solid coconut milk, cocoa powder, maple syrup, almond extract, lemon juice, oat milk, sunflower seed butter, salt, cashews and flax eggs and blend for a few minutes until the mixture is smooth and creamy and no cashew chunks remain.

Pour the filling over the crust and bake in the oven for 50 to 60 minutes. The outside edges will look done and the center will still be slightly jiggly; it will set up once it cools. Allow the cheesecake to cool to room temperature.

(continued)

YIELD: *8–10 servings*

CHEESECAKE FILLING

1¾ cups (255 g) raw cashews

5 tbsp (35 g) flaxseed meal

¾ cup (180 ml) water

½ cup (108 g) vegan butter

1 (13.5-oz [400-ml]) can coconut milk, solid part only

⅓ cup (32 g) unsweetened cocoa powder

1 cup (240 ml) maple syrup

1 tsp pure almond extract

2 tbsp (30 ml) lemon juice

¼ cup (60 ml) oat milk (or other plant milk)

¼ cup (63 g) sunflower seed butter (or other nut or seed butter)

Pinch of salt

CRUST

1 cup (80 g) gluten-free quick oats

⅓ cup (32 g) almond flour

⅓ cup (32 g) unsweetened cocoa powder

⅓ cup (43 g) coconut sugar

1 tsp cinnamon

Pinch of salt

3 tbsp (42 g) coconut oil, melted

½ tsp pure vanilla extract

BAKED CHOCOLATE
GANACHE CHEESECAKE (CONT.)

While the cheesecake is cooling, make the chocolate ganache. In a medium saucepan, heat the milk over medium-high heat until it starts to slowly boil. Add the chocolate chips, salt and maple syrup (if using), and stir it with a whisk until the chocolate chips start to melt. Remove from the heat and continue to whisk until the ganache is smooth and creamy. Allow the ganache to cool and thicken slightly, then pour it over the cheesecake. Place the cheesecake in the fridge to finish cooling overnight.

Keep leftover cheesecake stored in an airtight container in the fridge for up to 3 days.

NOTE: *If you prefer a more saucy ganache topping as opposed to a more set-up ganache, make the ganache right before serving and pour over the cheesecake, then serve.*

CHOCOLATE GANACHE

1¼ cups (300 ml) oat milk (or other plant milk, but do not use full-fat coconut milk)

1⅓ cups (223 g) dark chocolate chips

Pinch of salt

1 to 2 tbsp (15 to 30 ml) maple syrup (optional)

CREAMSICLE TART

This easy summer-inspired dessert tastes just like a creamsicle! I've taken one of America's favorite popsicle flavors and turned it into an easy gluten-free, grain-free, vegan tart that features a shortbread crust filled with a layer of vanilla coconut cream and topped with a cara cara orange citrus layer for the most refreshing, lower-sugar treat. Garnish the tart with vegan, dairy-free whipped cream and fresh orange slices and enjoy a little slice of summer!

Preheat your oven to 350°F (175°C). Spray a 9-inch (23-cm) tart pan with coconut oil. To make the crust, in a large bowl, whisk the flour and salt together, then add in the vanilla and agave or maple syrup. Knead in the butter with your hands or a pastry cutter until your dough forms. The dough should be slightly crumbly, but it should stick together between your fingers if you squeeze it. If it doesn't, add a little water.

Press the dough into the tart pan, starting with the outer edge, then press the remaining dough into the bottom of the tart pan. Smooth and press it down with the back of a spoon. You may have leftover crust, which you can use to make cookies (they're delicious!). Be sure not to fill the tart pan with too much dough so you leave room for the filling. Bake for 20 to 25 minutes, until the edges start to turn slightly golden. Do not overbake! You also may need to press down the crust lightly after you take it out of the oven with the back of a bowl or spoon to make a deeper well for the filling. Set the crust aside to cool while you make the coconut cream layer.

In a medium saucepan, whisk together the milk, agave or maple syrup, agar agar powder and salt. Cook the mixture on high heat and bring to a boil, whisking frequently. Remove from the heat and allow it to cool slightly.

(continued)

YIELD: *6–8 servings*

SHORTBREAD CRUST

2½ cups (305 g) cassava flour

1 tsp salt

1 tsp pure vanilla extract

½ cup (120 ml) agave or maple syrup

1 cup (215 g) vegan butter

COCONUT CREAM LAYER

1 (13.5-oz [400-ml]) can coconut milk

⅓ cup (80 ml) agave or maple syrup

1 tsp agar agar powder

Pinch of salt

CREAMSICLE TART
(CONT.)

To start the cara cara orange layer, peel the oranges and slice them in half. Add them to a blender with about ¼ cup (60 ml) of water. Blend on high until smooth. Strain the orange juice through a sieve or a nut milk bag to remove all the pulp and set aside. You should have about 1½ cups (360 ml) of cara cara orange juice.

Reserve ¼ cup (57 g) of the coconut cream mixture and set aside, then pour the rest of the coconut cream mixture into the tart shell. Carefully place the tart in your fridge for about 45 minutes, until the layer is firm to the touch.

In a medium saucepan, heat the orange juice, agave or maple syrup, almond extract, agar agar powder and ¼ cup (57 g) of the reserved coconut cream mixture over high heat and bring to a boil, whisking frequently. Set aside to cool slightly, then pour over top of the coconut cream layer in the tart. Place the tart back in the fridge to chill for about 4 hours or overnight. Keep the leftover tart stored in an airtight container in the fridge.

If using, make the whipped cream by spooning the solid part of the coconut milk into your mixing bowl. Whip it on high speed (either with a stand or hand mixer) until the coconut cream fluffs.

Mix the agar agar powder with water, then add it to the coconut cream along with the vanilla and sugar. Beat on high again for another few minutes, then place it in the fridge for 15 to 20 minutes. Using a piping bag and tip, pipe the whipped cream over the top of the tart or just slather it on! You can make the whipped cream a day ahead of time and keep it stored in the fridge until ready to use. You will need to let it warm slightly before piping or spreading.

CARA CARA ORANGE LAYER

6 cara cara oranges

½ cup (120 ml) agave or maple syrup

1 tsp pure almond extract

2 tsp (16 g) agar agar powder

WHIPPED CREAM (OPTIONAL)

2 (13.5-oz [400-ml]) cans coconut milk, solid part only

2 tsp (16 g) agar agar powder

6 tbsp (90 ml) water

1 tsp pure vanilla extract

½ cup (60 g) confectioners' sugar

CHOCOLATE COCOA CRUNCH BARS

These Chocolate Cocoa Crunch Bars remind me of chocolate-covered Rice Krispies Treats®, and they are definitely on my list of top favorite desserts in this book! While they are simple to make, these bars have just the right amount of crunch, sweetness and chocolate to keep you saying "Mmm" with every crispy bite.

Line an 8 x 8–inch (20 x 20–cm) baking pan with parchment paper. Place the cereal into a large bowl and set aside.

In a glass measuring cup or bowl, combine the tapioca syrup, oil, vanilla and peanut butter and melt in the microwave for 45 seconds to 1 minute. Stir the ingredients until completely melted and smooth. Pour the mixture into the bowl with the cereal and gently stir the cereal until it's evenly coated. Press the mixture into the baking pan, packing it down tightly. Place the pan in the fridge and chill for about 30 minutes.

Remove the block of cereal from the baking pan and place it onto a cutting board. Cut it into twelve evenly sized bars. Prepare a baking sheet with parchment paper and set aside.

To make the chocolate coating, melt the chocolate chips and oil together in a microwave-safe bowl until melted and smooth; stir to combine. I like to use a bowl large enough to be able to place the bars right into to coat with the chocolate.

Coat each bar fully with chocolate and, using a fork, let the excess chocolate drip off back into the bowl, then place the coated bar onto a parchment paper–lined baking sheet. Once all of the bars are covered in chocolate, place the baking sheet into the fridge to let the chocolate firm up before eating.

NOTE: You may use non-cocoa cereal if you can't find it, and even granola works for this recipe too!

YIELD: *12 bars*

BARS

4 cups (120 g) gluten-free cocoa brown rice cereal (see Note)

½ cup (120 ml) tapioca syrup

¼ cup (55 g) coconut oil

1 tsp pure vanilla extract

2 tbsp (32 g) unsweetened peanut butter (or other nut or seed butter)

CHOCOLATE COATING

2 cups (336 g) dark chocolate chips

1 tbsp (14 g) coconut oil

COCONUT
MACAROONS

Coconut is pretty prevalent in this book, from coconut milk and coconut oil to coconut flour and coconut sugar. This recipe incorporates all of the above for a coconut lover's dream dessert!

Preheat the oven to 325°F (160°C). In a small saucepan, bring the aquafaba to a boil and let it reduce for 5 to 7 minutes. Pour the reduced ¼ cup (60 ml) of aquafaba in the bowl of a stand mixer, add the cream of tartar and, using the whisk attachment, beat on high speed for 10 minutes, until stiff peaks form. Alternatively, you can do this with a hand blender on high speed.

In a large bowl, combine the coconut flakes, salt, flour and sugar and stir to combine. Once the aquafaba looks like whipped egg whites, gently pour the coconut mixture into the bowl with the aquafaba, add the vanilla and solid coconut milk and stir to form a batter.

Using a small cookie scoop (I used a #40), very tightly pack in some batter and plop it onto a parchment paper–lined baking sheet. You may also use a tablespoon, just form the batter into tightly packed balls. Bake the macaroons for 25 minutes. Remove from the oven and allow them to cool completely. They will be very crumbly if you try to touch them or move them once they come out of the oven, but they will set up as they cool.

If desired, make the chocolate drizzle by melting the chocolate chips and oil together for 45 seconds to 1 minute in the microwave, then drizzle the melted chocolate over top of each macaroon. Place them into the fridge to continue to set up completely for at least 2 hours.

YIELD: *12 macaroons*

MACAROONS

½ cup (120 ml) aquafaba

¼ tsp cream of tartar

2 cups (186 g) unsweetened coconut flakes

¼ tsp salt

¼ cup (28 g) coconut flour

¼ cup (33 g) coconut sugar

1 tsp pure vanilla extract

¼ cup (57 g) coconut milk, solid part only

CHOCOLATE DRIZZLE (OPTIONAL)

½ cup (84 g) dark chocolate chips

1 tsp coconut oil

WHITE CHOCOLATE PEANUT BUTTER CUPS

Dairy-free white chocolate does exist, but it's pretty hard to come by, so making your own white chocolate substitute at home is the way to go. Making your own white chocolate at home is also a good way to monitor just how much sweetener is used and to control what kind of sweetener is incorporated in the recipe. The white chocolate used in this recipe isn't "true" white chocolate, but it's a pretty darn good replacement and works perfectly in these peanut butter cups. These cups are simple to make and the best creamy snack to keep in your freezer for when the craving hits.

Line a mini muffin tin with liners. To make the white chocolate, melt the coconut cream, coconut oil, butter, maple syrup, vanilla, milk powder and salt in a glass measuring cup or bowl and stir to combine. Place ½ tablespoon (8 ml) of the white chocolate in the bottom of each mini muffin cup, then place into the freezer until firm, about 1 hour. Set the remaining white chocolate aside to use for the top layer.

While the bottom layer is setting up, make the peanut butter filling by stirring the peanut butter and tapioca syrup together until a dough forms.

Using a teaspoon, scoop a small (not heaping) teaspoon full of peanut butter filling into each muffin cup. Gently flatten the peanut butter "dough" so that it's just below the top of the muffin cup, leaving a small border around the edges so that the top layer of white chocolate can surround the peanut butter.

Stir the remaining white chocolate (remelt it if needed), then pour the remaining white chocolate over top of the peanut butter layer, and place the tin back into the freezer for a couple of hours until firm.

NOTE: *These melt very quickly, so enjoy right away and keep them stored in the freezer.*

YIELD: *12 cups*

WHITE CHOCOLATE
½ cup (114 g) coconut cream
2 tbsp (27 g) coconut oil
½ cup (120 g) coconut butter
¼ cup (60 ml) maple syrup
1 tsp pure vanilla extract
½ cup (48 g) coconut milk powder
Pinch of salt

PEANUT BUTTER FILLING
¼ cup (65 g) unsweetened peanut butter
½ tbsp (8 ml) tapioca syrup

STRAWBERRY BANANA BEET
NICE CREAM

Have you heard of nice cream? No, it's not a typo. I first discovered nice cream a couple of years ago and was so amazed by it, I just had to introduce you to one of my favorite nice cream flavor combos. Basically, nice cream is blended frozen fruit, most commonly using bananas as the base to give this frozen dessert a creamy texture similar to ice cream. Now I know you're thinking, "Beet?! Ew." But I promise this nice cream doesn't taste like beets but packs all the benefits beets have to offer. You'll want to make sure to freeze your fruit the day before, but other than that, this is an almost immediate healthy sweet treat!

YIELD: *4–6 servings*

2 frozen bananas

1 cup (166 g) frozen strawberries, diced

3 tbsp (45 ml) plant milk

2 tbsp (30 ml) agave syrup

½ tsp almond extract

1 tsp beet powder

Peel the bananas and break them into fourths. Place the banana pieces into a plastic bag and freeze overnight. Wash and dice the strawberries and place them into a separate plastic bag and freeze overnight.

The next day, place the plant milk, agave syrup, almond extract and beet powder in a food processor or blender. Add the frozen banana and strawberries and process until you achieve a smooth, ice cream–like texture. Serve in bowls or cones! This nice cream is best enjoyed right away, but you can also freeze any leftover nice cream; just allow it to slightly soften before you dig in.

CITRUS POPPY SEED
LOAF CAKE

This Citrus Poppy Seed Loaf Cake is so moist and delicious I almost called it a pound cake because it reminds me of such. I made mine a lemon loaf, but you can use any citrus you'd like. A blood orange poppy seed loaf would be amazing too! Besides being gluten-free and vegan, this loaf is also grain-free. If you prefer to swap out the regular sugar for coconut sugar that would be fine, but your loaf will be darker in color. Either way, deliciousness is at the forefront of this recipe!

Preheat the oven to 350°F (175°C). In a small bowl, combine the flaxseed meal and water to make flax eggs and set it aside. In another bowl, combine the plant milk with the vinegar and set aside to create a vegan buttermilk.

In a large bowl, combine the flours, baking powder, baking soda and poppy seeds.

In a separate large bowl, beat together the butter and sugar until creamy, then add the vanilla, flax eggs, milk mixture and citrus juice.

Using a spatula or spoon, combine the flour mixture with the wet mixture and stir just enough to form a batter. Do not overmix. Spoon the batter into a greased standard 8½ x 4½ x 2½–inch (22 x 12 x 6–cm) loaf pan and bake for 45 to 50 minutes. Let the loaf cool completely before icing.

To make the icing, whisk together the sugar and citrus juice to form a thick paste, then pour over the loaf. Let the icing harden before slicing and enjoying.

NOTE: *If you use a darker citrus juice, like blood orange, the batter color might vary.*

YIELD: *10 slices*

LOAF CAKE

4 tbsp (28 g) flaxseed meal

⅔ cup (160 ml) water

1 cup (240 ml) plant milk

1 tsp apple cider vinegar

1 cup (122 g) cassava flour

½ cup (48 g) almond flour

½ cup (56 g) coconut flour

2 tsp (9 g) baking powder

½ tsp baking soda

1½ tbsp (14 g) poppy seeds

½ cup (108 g) vegan butter, softened

½ cup (100 g) sugar (may substitute with coconut sugar)

1 tsp pure vanilla extract

¼ cup (60 ml) citrus juice (lemon, orange, grapefruit, etc.)

CITRUS ICING

1 cup (120 g) confectioners' sugar

2 tbsp (30 ml) citrus juice (lemon, orange, grapefruit, etc.)

APRICOT PIE POPS

The only thing better than a homemade pie is an adorable mini pie on a stick! Aside from them being undeniably cute, you don't have to share your pie pop with anyone, and absolutely no judgment if you have more than one. They are simple to make and perfect for any occasion. You can fill them with any fruit filling, but for this recipe, I chose to use apricots!

YIELD: *8–10 pops*

APRICOT FILLING

2 cups (450 g) apricots, skin off and pitted

½ tbsp (8 ml) lemon juice

2 tbsp (30 ml) maple syrup

1 tbsp (8 g) tapioca starch or arrowroot powder

CRUST

1 cup (96 g) almond flour

½ cup (56 g) coconut flour

½ cup (65 g) tapioca starch

½ tsp cinnamon

½ tsp baking powder

1 tsp salt

⅓ cup (80 ml) maple syrup

⅓ cup (80 g) coconut oil or vegan butter, melted

1 tsp pure vanilla extract

Lollipop sticks

Coconut oil, preferably spray coconut oil

To make the filling, place the apricots in a medium-large saucepan. Add the lemon juice, maple syrup and tapioca starch or arrowroot powder and heat over medium heat until the apricots start to reduce and the filling thickens. Be sure to stir frequently to avoid sticking to the bottom of the pan. While the apricots are simmering, make the crust.

In a large bowl, whisk together the flours, tapioca starch, cinnamon, baking powder and salt. Next, add the maple syrup, oil or butter and vanilla, and stir with a spatula or spoon until a dough forms. Place the dough onto a large piece of parchment paper, then place another piece of parchment paper on top of the dough and roll the dough out to ¼-inch (6-mm) thickness. Using a round cookie cutter or even a glass, cut rounds from the dough and place half of them onto a parchment paper–lined baking sheet. Preheat the oven to 375°F (190°C).

Lightly press one lollipop stick halfway up each round. Be gentle; you want the stick to stick, but not poke through the dough. If you're worried about the lollipop stick sticking, you can place a small piece of dough over top of the stick to secure it in place.

Next, place 1 teaspoon of the apricot mixture in the center of each round, almost to the edges but leaving a border. Using another small cookie cutter or a glass, cut out the center of the remaining pie rounds to allow the pies to vent while baking. Alternatively, you can just poke them with a fork. Place the cookie-cut dough round on top of the filling and gently press the top and bottom rounds together to seal the edges of the dough.

Spray the tops of the pie pops with coconut oil, then bake them in the oven for 18 to 20 minutes until they start to turn golden. Allow them to cool before enjoying. Store uncovered on your counter for up to 3 days.

NOTE: *To save on time, you may also use apricot preserves, but I recommend making your own!*

Hold The
DAIRY & BUTTER

Nondairy food products have come such a long way over the last five or so years. There are so many great options out there that fit into a dairy-free and/or vegan lifestyle. While I use dairy and butter replacements in almost all of the recipes in this book, I chose these specific recipes to be assigned to this section because I wanted to show just how easy it is to make a simple dairy swap with the available plant-based substitutions now available.

Vegan or Plant-Based Butter
There are many dairy-free, plant-based, vegan butter options available now! They taste great and can be used as a 1:1 replacement for regular butter in your recipes that help contribute to the texture in your baked goods, and they also offer that same richness real butter provides.

PRO: There are many great-tasting, readily available options now!

CON: Some contain soy, and all are made from oil, so if you're avoiding soy or oils, try using another swap.

Aquafaba
Using the liquid/brine from a can of unsalted chickpeas (salted brine doesn't work!) is one of my favorite baking secrets! As well as being a stellar egg replacement, it's a great go-to for dairy-free baking as well. Because it whips up so well, like egg whites, you can actually use it to make marshmallow fluff, frosting, butter or whipped cream. It's perfect for meringue and macarons too!

PROS: It's inexpensive and readily available from a can of chickpeas! It whips up perfectly, like magic, and it makes a fantastic replacement for both dairy and eggs.

CON: It does deflate when combined with other wet ingredients, so that can prove to be tricky sometimes.

Coconut Milk

The creamiest of all of the milk replacements is coconut milk. I find it to be my favorite when I am looking for a richer dessert. You can buy it in the canned section, usually the international food aisle, at your local grocery store, or even online too. Some recipes call for just the solid cream part only, so be sure to pay attention to that. You can buy coconut milk in full-fat or light versions; I tend to stick with the full-fat, as I find it works better in dessert recipes, whereas the light coconut milk works best in savory dishes. Coconut milk also allows for the dessert to firm up a bit more than another plant-based milk would because it becomes more solid when chilled.

PRO: It's thick and creamy, perfect for making no-churn, dairy-free ice cream, caramel or mousse, but it can also be used as a 1:1 replacement for milk in cakes, brownies, cookies, etc.

CON: Sometimes it leaves your desserts with a coconut-infused flavor, so if you don't like the taste of coconut, you might want to opt for another dairy-free milk.

Coconut Butter

Coconut butter is different from coconut oil, as it's made from grinding the flesh of the coconut. Because it's thicker and more flavorful than coconut oil, it's a lot richer and can provide your desserts with that rich, creamy flavor without using real butter.

PRO: You can try making your own at home—it's super easy! Just blend unsweetened coconut in your food processor until smooth!

CON: It's a bit expensive and hard to find, and it does give your desserts a more coconutty flavor.

Coconut Oil

Coconut oil has been getting a lot of attention lately as a great go-to replacement for butter and oil that is full of MCTs (medium-chain triglycerides) instead of saturated fats, giving your brain and body an energy boost. While that is true, it's still an oil and may not want to be used in excess.

PRO: Coconut oil is used as a 1:1 replacement for dairy butter. When used solid (not melted coconut oil) in pie crust, it offers a flakier crust.

CON: Because coconut oil hardens when cold, storing desserts that use coconut oil in the fridge can decrease their fluffiness and make them hard. You can store desserts made with coconut oil covered tightly on your counter for up to 2 days or freeze them to enjoy later.

Coconut Milk Powder

Coconut milk powder is evaporated coconut milk, just like the regular evaporated milk you might be used to, but it's a nonliquid ingredient. When used in its powdered form, it does add creaminess.

PROS: It makes your desserts very creamy and can be used in beverages (think hot chocolate or coffee!) too. It can be used to make coconut milk in a pinch by adding 3 tablespoons (27 g) of coconut milk powder to 1 cup (240 ml) of hot water.

CON: There are only a couple of brands that make it, and it might just be easier to use coconut milk as a liquid replacement.

Nut, Seed or Grain Milk

Nut, seed or grain milk can be used as a 1:1 replacement for dairy milk in your baking recipes. Some plant milks are creamier than others, so it's really up to you on which swap you like best. I usually use oat milk, coconut milk, almond milk or flax milk.

PROS: There are tons of dairy milk replacements made from nuts and seeds that are readily available at most grocery stores now! This is great for those with lactose intolerance or those who do better on a dairy-free diet. You can also make your own plant milk at home with your blender and a nut milk bag or cheesecloth, water, your chosen nut or seed, salt and maybe maple syrup.

CON: Some of these replacements can be a tad watery and/or have added sugars and gums. Be sure to read the ingredients and nutrition labels to decide which you'd like best. I usually opt for unsweetened milk replacements with minimal ingredients.

Dairy-Free Unsweetened Yogurt

For dessert recipes that call for yogurt, you can now buy many different types of dairy-free yogurt at the store! There's yogurt made from nuts, coconuts, oats and even soy.

PRO: It's readily available at most grocery stores now, and they taste pretty great!

CON: Some of the store-bought yogurts (just like some of the dairy yogurts) have a high sugar content. If you're trying to be more mindful of that, maybe make your own dairy-free yogurt at home. It's a lot simpler than you think!

Dairy-Free Cream Cheese

For dessert recipes that call for cream cheese, you can now buy these products at the store, and they are a great alternative to real dairy cream cheese. Sometimes using cashews or tofu for vegan cheesecake recipes is another common swap.

PRO: It's readily available at most grocery stores now!

CON: Some of them don't taste that great or would not be a good choice in a dessert recipe, and some are made with soy. If you're avoiding soy, this might not be the best option.

SALTED CARAMEL
FUDGE

This Salted Caramel Fudge is one of the easiest dessert recipes in this book; you'll be making it over and over! Simply take my vegan caramel recipe, pour it into your favorite mold, sprinkle it with sea salt and keep this melt-in-your-mouth fudge chilled in your fridge for when the mood hits.

In a small saucepan, melt the vegan butter or oil over high heat. Once melted, whisk in the solid coconut cream and maple syrup. Whisking continuously, add the almond or sunflower seed butter and continue to whisk until the mixture starts to thicken, 3 to 5 minutes. Turn the heat to low and whisk in the vanilla and salt.

Pour the caramel into a silicone candy mold. Alternatively, you can pour it into a mini muffin tin lined with mini muffin cups. Garnish with sea salt, then chill in the fridge until set, about 30 minutes. Keep the fudge stored in an airtight container in the fridge for about 2 weeks or in the freezer.

YIELD: *6–8 servings*

½ cup (108 g) vegan butter or coconut oil

2 tbsp (30 g) coconut cream

½ cup (120 ml) maple syrup

5 tbsp (80 g) almond butter, or sunflower seed butter for nut-free

1 tsp pure vanilla extract

Pinch of salt

Coarse or large flake sea salt, for garnishing

BOURBON PEACH
ICE CREAM

Adding bourbon to my desserts is a newfound love of mine! It adds such a deep, rich flavor—especially when paired with the peaches, cinnamon and vanilla in this ice cream recipe. But if you want to make this recipe kid-friendly, you can simply omit the bourbon. For simplicity, I used canned peaches in this recipe, but you can certainly use fresh peaches, just be sure to peel them first.

In a saucepan over medium heat, whisk together the solid coconut milk, peaches, vanilla, maple syrup, arrowroot powder, bourbon (if using) and cinnamon until smooth and creamy. Pour the mixture into ice cube trays and freeze overnight.

The next day, place the ice cream cubes in a blender and blend until you achieve a creamy ice cream texture, adding a splash of plant milk if needed (but not too much!). Enjoy immediately and place the remaining ice cream in an airtight container and store in the freezer.

NOTES: *After freezing the leftover ice cream, allow the ice cream to sit out for about 5 minutes to soften just a bit before enjoying. Also, be sure to use a gluten-free bourbon. If you can't find gluten-free bourbon, you can certainly omit the bourbon from this recipe and the peach ice cream is still delicious!*

YIELD: *6–8 servings*

1 (13.5-oz [400-ml]) can coconut milk, solid part only

2 cups (570 g) peaches, peeled (may use canned if desired)

2 tsp (10 ml) pure vanilla extract

⅓ cup (80 ml) maple syrup

1 tbsp (8 g) arrowroot powder

2 tbsp (30 ml) bourbon (see Notes)

⅛ tsp cinnamon

Plant milk, if needed

BROWNED BUTTER
CARAMEL POPCORN

If you're looking for the next sweet snack to serve at all your parties, look no further! Homemade browned butter caramel gets drizzled over freshly popped popcorn and then baked to crispy snacking perfection! This gluten-free, vegan Browned Butter Caramel Popcorn is so easy to make and will definitely be all the rave at your next get-together.

Preheat your oven to 300°F (150°C). Pop the popcorn per the package instructions. Set aside. Prepare a large parchment paper–lined baking sheet and set aside.

Heat a small saucepan over medium-high heat and melt the butter, whisking occasionally, until it starts to turn golden brown. Once the butter is browned, add the maple syrup, tapioca syrup, vanilla and salt. Whisk to combine. Lower the heat and, while continuously whisking, add the sunflower seed butter. Keep whisking until it thickens, 3 to 5 minutes. Add the solid coconut milk and whisk. Lastly, add the baking soda, and be careful, as it will bubble up slightly. Continue to whisk for a couple of minutes until you have a very smooth caramel sauce. Remove from the heat and allow it to cool slightly.

Split the popcorn into two large bowls. Pour ½ cup (120 ml) of the caramel over each batch of popcorn and gently stir to coat the popcorn with the caramel, then spread the popcorn on the baking trays.

Use the remaining caramel to drizzle over top of the popcorn, if desired, and bake for 25 to 30 minutes. Remove from the oven and let it cool slightly, then take the popcorn off the tray to cool completely (this will make it crispier). Break apart the popcorn or leave it as chunks. Store the popcorn uncovered on your counter for up to 1 day or, for crispier popcorn, you can store it in your fridge for up to 3 days.

YIELD: *about 12 cups of caramel popcorn*

½ cup (107 g) unpopped popcorn kernels

BROWNED BUTTER CARAMEL SAUCE

6 tbsp (84 g) vegan butter

3 tbsp (45 ml) maple syrup

2 tbsp (30 ml) tapioca syrup

½ tsp pure vanilla extract

Pinch of salt

2 tbsp (32 g) sunflower seed butter

3 tbsp (45 g) coconut milk, solid part only

½ tsp baking soda

FUDGESICLES

Skip the store-bought fudgesicles and make these healthier pops at home! They are so quick and easy to make, you can make them the night before, freeze and enjoy the next day. You can choose to drizzle them with chocolate sauce or just enjoy this creamy dessert as is. Give this frozen treat a superfood boost and garnish it with raw cacao nibs.

In a small saucepan, heat the milk over medium heat, whisking frequently. Whisk in the cocoa powder, maple syrup, vanilla and salt until smooth and creamy.

For ease of getting them into the freezer, place popsicle molds on a baking sheet. Pour the mixture into the popsicle molds, insert the popsicle sticks and freeze for 4 hours, or preferably overnight. Store in the freezer and enjoy within a few days.

If decorating with drizzled chocolate, melt chocolate chips with coconut oil in the microwave and then drizzle the melted chocolate over the fudgesicles with a spoon. Garnish with raw cacao nibs, if desired.

YIELD: *4–6 fudgesicles*

1 (13.5-oz [400-ml]) can coconut milk

3 tbsp (15 g) unsweetened cocoa powder

¼ cup (60 ml) maple syrup

1 tsp pure vanilla extract

Pinch of salt

CHOCOLATE DRIZZLE (OPTIONAL)

3 tbsp (45 g) vegan dark chocolate chips

1 tsp coconut oil

Raw cacao nibs (optional)

"TWIX" TART

Channel your inner chocolate lover with this rich, silky, decadent Twix®-esque tart! You can pipe extra chocolate mousse on top for the perfect finishing touch.

Preheat your oven to 350°F (175°C). Spray a 9-inch (23-cm) tart pan with coconut oil. In a large bowl, whisk together the flour and salt, then add the vanilla and maple syrup and stir to combine. Then, knead in the butter with your hands until a dough forms. Press the crust into the prepared tart pan, starting with the outside of the tart first, then pressing the remaining dough into the bottom of the tart pan. If you have leftover dough, you can use it to make cookies or freeze for a recipe later on. Using a fork, poke holes in the bottom of the tart, then bake for 20 to 25 minutes, until the edges start to turn slightly golden.

While the crust is baking, make the caramel layer. In a small saucepan, melt the butter over high heat. Once melted, whisk in the maple syrup. Then whisk in the solid coconut milk. Whisking continuously, add the sunflower seed butter and continue to whisk until the mixture starts to thicken, 3 to 5 minutes. Turn the heat to low and whisk in the vanilla and salt. Remove from the heat and continue to whisk for a minute or so, then let it cool until the crust finishes baking.

Remove the crust from the oven and allow it to slightly cool. You may need to gently press down the bottom of the crust, then pour the caramel into the crust and place the tart into the fridge to chill for about 20 minutes.

While the caramel layer is setting up, make the chocolate mousse layer. Heat the milk, chocolate, maple syrup, oil and salt in a saucepan until the chocolate is melted and the mixture is simmering, but not boiling. Whisk frequently until smooth and glossy. Remove the chocolate mixture from the heat and allow it to cool for 10 to 15 minutes, then pour it over top of the caramel layer in the tart. Allow the tart to cool to room temperature, then place it carefully back into the fridge for at least 4 to 6 hours, preferably overnight, to fully set up.

You will likely have leftover chocolate mousse, so simply pour it into a container and also chill it in the fridge overnight. Then, you can pipe it onto your tart the next day. Once the tart is set, pipe any leftover chocolate mousse in any design you wish.

YIELD: *6–8 servings*

SHORTBREAD CRUST

3 cups (366 g) cassava flour

½ tsp salt

1½ tsp (8 ml) pure vanilla extract

½ cup (120 ml) maple syrup

½ cup (108 g) vegan butter

CARAMEL LAYER

3 tbsp (42 g) vegan butter (may substitute with coconut oil instead if you wish)

2 tbsp (30 ml) maple syrup

2 tbsp (30 g) coconut milk, solid part only

2 tbsp (32 g) sunflower seed butter

¼ tsp pure vanilla extract

Pinch of salt

CHOCOLATE MOUSSE LAYER

1 (13.5-oz [400-ml]) can coconut milk

8 oz (226 g) dark chocolate

¼ cup (60 ml) maple syrup

¼ cup (60 g) coconut oil

½ tsp salt

FUNFETTI
SUGAR COOKIES

Giving birthday cake a run for its money, these easy funfetti sugar cookies are perfect for any occasion that calls for a rainbow celebration! They bake up with perfectly crispy outside edges and soft, chewy centers. I like to use naturally colored sprinkles that you can find online to keep these cookies dye-free.

YIELD: *11–12 cookies*

1 tbsp (7 g) flaxseed meal
3½ tbsp (53 ml) water, divided
½ cup (108 g) vegan butter
1 cup (192 g) organic cane sugar
1 tsp pure vanilla extract
1 tbsp (8 g) arrowroot powder
1⅔ cups (240 g) gluten-free baking flour
1 tsp baking soda
½ tsp cream of tartar
½ tsp salt
½ cup (144 g) rainbow sprinkles, preferably dye-free

Preheat the oven to 350°F (175°C). Line a baking sheet with parchment paper. Combine the flaxseed meal with 2½ tablespoons (38 ml) of water in a small bowl to make the flax egg and set it aside. In the bowl of a stand mixer fitted with the paddle attachment, cream together the butter and sugar on medium speed until creamy. Alternatively, you can use a hand mixer. Add the flax egg and vanilla and mix on low speed until fully incorporated. Combine the arrowroot powder with the remaining 1 tablespoon (15 ml) of water in a small bowl to form a paste, then add it to the bowl.

In a medium bowl, whisk together the flour, baking soda, cream of tartar and salt, then slowly add the dry ingredients into the wet ingredients. Mix on low speed until the cookie dough forms.

Remove the bowl from the stand mixer and gently fold in the sprinkles with a spatula or spoon. Tightly pack a medium-sized cookie scoop with dough to form the cookies, then place each cookie directly onto the prepared baking sheet. Flatten each cookie with your hand until it is about ¾ inch (2 cm) thick. Bake in the oven for 10 to 12 minutes. They will look underbaked but will set up more as they cool, and remember we want the chewy centers!

NOTE: *You can swap out the organic cane sugar for coconut sugar, but the cookie batter will be a darker color and the rainbow sprinkles may not show as much.*

BOOZY CHOCOLATE
TRUFFLES

These delicious little adult-only gems are perfect for your next evening soiree. They are simple to make and easy to please, a winning dessert combo if you ask me! I use Amaretto in these chocolate truffles, but you can also use brandy or another sweet liqueur, just make sure it's gluten-free friendly. You can also just leave the booze out of these truffles altogether and they will still be delicious and kid-friendly too. Sprinkle with sea salt for that salty-sweet combo we all love!

In a medium saucepan, melt the chocolate chips, coconut butter and milk over low heat. Once the chocolate chips start to melt, whisk continuously until you have a creamy melted chocolate. Add the Amaretto (if using) and whisk. Pour the mixture into a bowl and place in the fridge to set up for about an hour or overnight.

Once the chocolate is solid, use a small melon baller or a tablespoon to scoop the chocolate mixture into balls, rolling them between your hands to round them, if desired.

To make the chocolate shell, line a baking sheet with parchment paper. Melt the chocolate chips and coconut oil in a small bowl in the microwave for 30 seconds at a time until smooth. Roll the rounded truffles in the melted chocolate using a fork to make sure all sides are coated, then place the chocolate-covered truffles onto the prepared baking sheet. Roll them in finely chopped peanuts and/or cocoa powder or sprinkle with sea salt (my personal fave!), then place them onto a parchment paper–lined plate or in mini muffin cups and store them in the fridge.

NOTE: *You may swap the coconut butter for vegan butter, if desired.*

YIELD: *20–25 truffles*

TRUFFLES

1⅔ cups (252 g) dark chocolate chips, divided

3 tbsp (45 g) coconut butter (see Note)

4 tbsp (60 ml) plant milk

4 tbsp (60 ml) good-quality Amaretto (optional)

OUTER CHOCOLATE SHELL

¼ cup (42 g) dark chocolate chips

1 tsp coconut oil

TOPPING

Finely chopped peanuts

Unsweetened cocoa powder

Sea salt

Achieving the
PERFECT BATTER

I have been gluten-free for 7 years now, so it's getting a little bit fuzzy at this point, but traditionally when you bake, you like your batter very moist and almost runny. Gluten-free vegan baking is tricky in this way. It has taken me years of practice to figure out when my batter is the right consistency to bake to the right texture. I recently had that "aha" moment with the perfect batter, and now I'm sharing what I've learned with all of you! With gluten-free baking, you definitely want your batter to be more of a bready, doughlike texture. If it's not, the center won't bake and you'll end up with a sinkhole in the middle, only to realize it after it has cooled and it's too late to stick it back in the oven. Why yes, this has happened to me more than a few times. And on the other hand, you don't want your batter to be too dry, because then you have no moisture in your bakery at all and you'll just end up needing to wash it down with a tall glass of (plant) milk. Not at all satisfying.

When you take the gluten away, you lose that flexible binder that gives bread and baked desserts that pillowy softness, but don't worry, there are things we can "replace gluten" with to bring some of that back. Take the eggs away and the whole fluffy-rising thing that normally happens is gone too. Take the dairy butter and milk away and you lose some of the flakiness and browning you might see in "regular" baking. I know all of this seems disheartening, but don't worry. I've figured out a lot of great tricks to make up for it, ensuring that your batter is just the right consistency and your gluten-free vegan desserts taste great.

Luckily, there's gluten-free baking powder and baking soda to give your bakery a little volume back, so your pancakes aren't, well, flat as a pancake. There are great egg replacers and vegan butters to use now, and nut or seed butters can be used for a lot more than just to top your (gluten-free) sandwiches and toast. I'll touch on these points more in the next sections.

Let's go over a couple of batter-related problems and their solutions.

Problem Scenario #1: Your Bakery Is Too Gummy
This is not an uncommon mishap in gluten-free vegan baking. Maybe your pancakes aren't super fluffy like you like them. In that case, try lowering the heat and cooking them longer. My other suggestion would be to try a different flour. Something in the mixture is giving it that dense, gummy texture. It could be one of the "gums," like xanthan gum, for example. That's why I like to use a combination of flours instead of buying premixed all-purpose flours, unless you find one that works well.

Problem Scenario #2: You Have a Crumbly, Dry Texture
You most likely need more moisture. Seems like a simple fix, but remember we don't want to add too much or your bakery won't bake all the way through, and you'll end up with overdone edges and an uncooked center. I like to use nut butters to keep some moisture without making my batter too runny.

Problem Scenario #3: Dang It! That Center Is Still Mushy!
Try lowering the oven temperature next time and cooking the bakery for longer. You can also turn the oven off after the baking time is up and allow it to slowly cool in the oven to "dry it out" a bit more.

Problem Scenario #4: The Edges Are Too Tough and Crispy
Try lining your cake or loaf pan with parchment paper to cover the sides and the bottom, then bake.

Problem Scenario #5: Your Dessert Turned Out Hard as a Rock!
Try adding more egg replacement or ground psyllium husk, considered to be a "gluten-like" replacement. Also, add more baking powder or baking soda to help with leavening. I'll touch more on this in the powders section.

Once you start to notice which dessert recipes are turning out well, take note of how the batter looks before baking. You can then try to achieve a similar consistency for similar desserts.

How to Tell When It's Done

Sometimes, it can be hard to tell when gluten-free vegan bakery is done. You don't want to underbake, because you may end up with an undone center. But you also don't want to overbake, or it'll be crumbly and dry. You can use the toothpick method, but even sometimes that's not a foolproof way to tell if something is fully baked as the center will continue to set up as it cools. Generally, I would say 25 to 50 minutes is the appropriate time to bake. That seems like a big range, but if your batter is more spread out, you'll more likely bake in the 25- to 30-minute range.

Check the edges; are they getting crispy? If so, it's probably done. Can you smell it? If so, it's probably close to being done. Does it jiggle when you shake it? You probably need to bake it longer, unless noted otherwise in the instructions.

Gluten-free vegan baking will sometimes seem undone, but it just needs to set up a bit longer than traditional baked goods. I know you want that cake and want it now, but it takes patience, my friends. The recipes in this chapter have been quite the challenge for me to perfect. I've had lots of sunken-in-the-middle cakes, hard-as-a-rock brownies and dry, crumbly cookies, so join in the celebration that I've figured out just the right batter consistency for the following desserts!

FLOURLESS FUDGY BROWNIES

If you're a thin brownie lover, these brownies will rock your world! If you're a thick brownie lover, well, these flourless fudgy brownies are so delicious I think they may just sway you to Team Thin Brownie. They are crinkly on the top and around the edges and soft and fudgy in the middle—everything a brownie should be.

Preheat the oven to 350°F (175°C). Line an 8 x 8–inch (20 x 20–cm) baking pan with parchment paper and set aside. Next, beat the aquafaba in a large bowl with a beater until it turns foamy, 1 to 2 minutes. If you don't have a beater, whisk it by hand very quickly until it turns foamy. Add the chocolate chips and oil to a glass measuring cup or bowl and microwave for 1 minute, then stir. If all of the chocolate chips aren't melted and the mixture isn't smooth, microwave for another 30 seconds.

Add the tapioca starch, sugar, cocoa powder, baking powder, salt and melted chocolate to the bowl with the aquafaba and stir with a spatula until you have a smooth brownie batter. Pour the batter into the parchment paper–lined baking pan and bake in the oven for 20 to 25 minutes. Let the brownies cool completely before enjoying. Serve with a scoop of my No-Churn Vanilla Ice Cream, if desired!

YIELD: *9 brownies*

⅓ cup (80 ml) aquafaba

1 cup (168 g) dark chocolate chips

4 tbsp (60 ml) avocado oil

½ cup (65 g) tapioca starch

¾ cup (98 g) coconut sugar

¼ cup (22 g) unsweetened cocoa powder

1 tbsp (14 g) baking powder

Pinch of salt

No-Churn Vanilla Ice Cream (page 153), for serving (optional)

TURTLE THUMBPRINT COOKIES

Every year at Christmas, my parents would make a variety of cookies from recipes that have been passed down through the generations—one of my favorite holiday traditions. Thumbprint cookies were one of my favorite cookies of all the cookies we made. Although we would have normally put jam in the middle of these cookies, I decided to fill them with my Vegan Caramel Sauce (page 157), add pecans to the cookie batter and then sprinkle them with chocolate chunks to take these from thumbprint cookies to turtle thumbprint cookies. They got the approval of my parents, phew! So maybe now there's a new cookie on the traditional holiday list!

Preheat the oven to 350°F (175°C). Beat the butter until smooth, then add the sugar and beat until well combined. In a separate bowl, combine the flour, baking soda and salt, then slowly add it to the butter mixture, beating it until well combined. Turn the beater or mixer off and stir in the milk, oats and pecans. Using a #40 cookie scoop (or a tablespoon), scoop the cookie dough, then shape the portioned dough into balls. Place them 2 inches (5 cm) apart on an ungreased baking sheet.

Next, press down in the center of each cookie with your thumb and bake for 12 minutes. Remove from the oven and let them cool completely. You may need to gently press the center down again with the back of a measuring spoon to ensure the well is deep enough to fill.

Make the Vegan Caramel Sauce. Once the cookies are completely cool, spoon some caramel sauce into the middle of each cookie and garnish with chopped dark chocolate.

YIELD: *16–18 cookies*

COOKIES
½ cup (108 g) vegan butter, softened

¾ cup (98 g) coconut sugar

1¼ cups (150 g) oat flour

½ tsp baking soda

¼ tsp salt

2 tbsp (30 ml) plant milk

1 cup (80 g) gluten-free quick oats

½ cup (55 g) chopped pecans

TOPPINGS
Vegan Caramel Sauce (page 157)

Dark chocolate, chopped

PERFECTLY SPICED
CARROT CAKE

Carrot cake has always been one of the most popular cake flavors—hooray for sneaking in some real carrots! This carrot cake recipe uses a combination of flax eggs, plant butter, applesauce, nut butter and pumpkin puree to give it that oh-so-soft, melt-in-your-mouth cake texture. And whether you fully frost this cake or decide to go with the naked cake frosting method, I think you're going to fall in love with this recipe!

Preheat your oven to 350°F (175°C). Grease three 6-inch (15-cm) cake pans. Make your flax eggs first by combining the flaxseed meal and water in a small bowl and set it aside. In a large bowl, add the flour, sugar, baking powder, baking soda, cinnamon, nutmeg, ginger and salt, and whisk until combined. In the bowl of a stand mixer or a large bowl, add the butter, applesauce, cashew butter, maple syrup, pumpkin puree and vanilla. Using the stand mixer, an electric beater or mixing by hand, beat on low speed until well combined. Add the flax eggs. Slowly add the dry ingredients to the wet ingredients to form your cake batter. Turn the beater off, then stir in the carrots with a spatula. Evenly divide up the batter between the three pans. Bake in the oven for 30 minutes. Allow the cakes to cool for 10 minutes in the cake pans, then gently remove the cakes from the pans and place them on a cooling rack to cool completely, about 1 hour.

To make the buttercream frosting, beat the butter and vanilla until smooth and creamy, then add the cinnamon and sugar a little at a time. Beat until your buttercream is smooth.

Spread about one-quarter of the buttercream over the top of one cake, then place another cake on top. Spread another one-quarter of the buttercream over the top of that cake and top with the last cake. Frost the entire cake carefully until all the frosting is used. Piping is optional. Garnish with chopped walnuts, if desired. Keep stored in the fridge in an airtight container and let it warm slightly to room temperature before enjoying.

YIELD: *6–8 slices*

CAKE
3 tbsp (21 g) flaxseed meal

¼ cup (60 ml) water

2 cups (296 g) gluten-free baking flour

1 cup (130 g) coconut sugar

1 tbsp (14 g) baking powder

1 tsp baking soda

1 tbsp (8 g) cinnamon

¼ tsp ground nutmeg

¼ tsp ground ginger

¼ tsp salt

½ cup (108 g) vegan butter, softened

¼ cup (61 g) unsweetened applesauce

¼ cup (63 g) cashew butter

½ cup (120 ml) maple syrup

½ cup (123 g) pure pumpkin puree

2 tsp (10 ml) pure vanilla extract

2 cups (180 g) carrots, grated

BUTTERCREAM FROSTING
1 cup (215 g) vegan butter, softened

1 tsp pure vanilla extract

1 tsp cinnamon

4 cups (480 g) confectioners' sugar

TOPPING (OPTIONAL)
Chopped walnuts

CINNAMON CHURRO CUPCAKES

I knew I wanted to make something churro for this book. I do love churros, but I'm not the biggest fan of fried desserts, so I decided to make churro-flavored cupcakes, and oh my gosh, these exceeded my expectations! They taste just like cinnamon sugar churros! I think all you churro lovers will be swooning over these delicious cupcakes.

In a glass bowl or measuring cup, whisk together the milk, apple cider vinegar, vanilla, maple syrup and oil and let it sit for about 10 minutes.

Preheat oven to 350°F (175°C). In a large bowl, stir together the flours, salt, baking soda, baking powder and cinnamon, then add the milk mixture and stir just enough to form a batter. Line a cupcake pan and fill each liner to just below the top. Bake for 15 minutes, or until risen and a toothpick inserted into the center of a cupcake comes out clean. Let the cupcakes cool completely in the cupcake pan before frosting.

To make the cinnamon frosting, cream together the butter, shortening, vanilla and cinnamon with an electric mixer until smooth and creamy, then add the sugar, a little bit at a time. Transfer the frosting to a piping bag and frost the cupcakes. Store any leftover cupcakes on your counter for 1 day or covered in an airtight container for up to 3 days in your fridge.

YIELD: *8–9 cupcakes*

CUPCAKES
⅔ cup plus ½ cup (280 ml) almond milk

2 tsp (10 ml) apple cider vinegar

1 tsp pure vanilla extract

½ cup (120 ml) maple syrup

¼ cup (60 ml) avocado oil

½ cup (61 g) cassava flour

½ cup (48 g) almond flour

½ cup (56 g) coconut flour

¼ tsp salt

½ tsp baking soda

1 tsp baking powder

1 tsp cinnamon

CINNAMON FROSTING
½ cup (108 g) vegan butter

½ cup (103 g) vegan shortening

1 tsp pure vanilla extract

½ tsp cinnamon

1 cup (120 g) confectioners' sugar

VANILLA OAT
BISCOTTI

Growing up in an Italian home, we always had biscotti at holidays and family gatherings, but until this book, I've never actually made them. I called my dad over with his box of recipes and we settled on this simple family vanilla biscotti recipe—just converted to be gluten-free and vegan, using oat flour as the base. It took a couple of tries to get the batter just right, but we certainly are happy with how they turned out and we hope you like them too!

YIELD: *9–10 biscotti*

4 tbsp (28 g) flaxseed meal

⅔ cup (160 ml) water

¼ cup (54 g) vegan butter, softened

⅔ cup (86 g) coconut sugar

1 tsp pure vanilla extract

3 cups (360 g) oat flour

2 tsp (9 g) baking powder

1 tsp cinnamon

Preheat the oven to 350°F (175°C). Line a baking sheet with parchment paper. To make the flax eggs, combine the flaxseed meal and water in a small bowl and set it aside for about 5 minutes.

Using an electric beater, beat the butter, sugar and vanilla in a large bowl until smooth and creamy, then add in the flax eggs and mix to combine.

In a medium bowl, whisk together the flour, baking powder and cinnamon, then stir in the butter mixture; you may also use your hands.

Turn the dough out onto the prepared baking sheet and form the dough into a log measuring approximately 3 inches (8 cm) wide, 1½ inches (4 cm) thick and 10 inches (25 cm) long. Bake for 25 minutes, until firm. Remove from the oven and allow it to cool for about 30 minutes.

With a sharp knife, carefully slice the log diagonally into ¾-inch (2-cm)-thick slices. If it's too crumbly, allow it to cool for longer. Place the cut sides down on the same parchment paper–lined baking sheet and bake at 350°F (175°C) for an additional 10 to 12 minutes, then set the oven to broil and broil the biscotti for 5 to 7 minutes on each side, watching them very carefully so they don't burn. Store leftover biscotti on your counter *uncovered* for 3 to 4 days.

NOTE: *You may dip them in melted chocolate and allow the chocolate to harden before enjoying.*

SERIOUSLY EASY PUMPKIN PIE

This traditional holiday favorite is too good not to include in this book! You may only make this dessert once a year, but if you're feeling particularly nostalgic, this pumpkin pie is sure to give you those cozy holiday feelings all year round. With simple, gluten-free and vegan ingredients, I've taken a classic and made it available for all to enjoy! Even my pumpkin pie-loving, non-vegan or gluten-free mother-in-law said it is a "marvelous pumpkin pie!" Now that's something to be thankful for!

Preheat the oven to 350°F (175°C). Grease a standard 9-inch (23-cm) pie plate with butter or spray coconut oil. To make the crust, whisk together the flours, salt and sugar (if using) in a large bowl. Next, add both the oil and butter and knead the dough with your hands or a pastry cutter. Add the water and continue to knead until your pie dough can roll into a ball. Press the dough into the sides of the greased pie plate first, then press the rest of the dough into the bottom of the pie plate. Reserve some pie crust if you wish to make leaf cutouts for the top, but this is completely optional.

To make the filling, in a large bowl, add the pumpkin puree, solid coconut milk, vanilla, tapioca starch, sugar, cloves, cinnamon, allspice, nutmeg and salt, and mix all the ingredients together. Alternatively, you can add all the filling ingredients to a blender and blend until combined. Pour the pumpkin mixture into the pie crust and use a spatula to spread the pumpkin filling evenly and smooth out the top. Bake for 45 to 50 minutes. When you remove it from the oven, the edges might look done and the middle may still look wobbly. This is fine; it will set up as it cools. Chill the pumpkin pie uncovered in the fridge overnight until completely set. Serve with coconut whipped topping and sprinkle with cinnamon, if desired.

To make the pie crust leaves, reserve some of the pie crust (or if you like a lot of leaves, make a new batch of pie dough) and roll or flatten out the dough to about ½ inch (1.3 cm) thick. Transfer the leaf cutouts to a parchment paper–lined baking sheet, brush them with plant milk and bake them at 350°F (175°C) for 25 to 30 minutes. Let them cool before placing them on top of the pumpkin pie.

YIELD: *6–8 slices*

CRUST

2 cups (296 g) gluten-free baking flour

½ cup (56 g) coconut flour

1 tsp salt

2 tbsp (16 g) coconut or date sugar (optional)

⅓ cup (80 g) coconut oil, softened but not completely melted

½ cup (108 g) vegan butter

6 to 7 tbsp (90 to 105 ml) water, ice cold

FILLING

1 (15-oz [425-g]) can pure pumpkin puree

1 (13.5-oz [400-ml]) can coconut milk, solid part only

2 tsp (10 ml) pure vanilla extract

¼ cup (33 g) tapioca starch

1 cup (130 g) coconut sugar

⅛ tsp ground cloves

1 tsp cinnamon

¼ tsp allspice

¼ tsp nutmeg

½ tsp salt

TOPPINGS (OPTIONAL)

Coconut whipped topping

Cinnamon

Pie leaves from leftover pie crust

CINNAMON ROLL
COOKIES

If you thought cinnamon rolls couldn't get any better, say hello to Cinnamon Roll Cookies! They taste like cinnamon rolls without all of the work that comes along with them. There's no rise time and no long baking time. The soft cookie dough is made with simple ingredients and then rolled with a date sugar filling and baked for just 12 minutes. Frost with vegan cream cheese frosting for melt-in-your-mouth deliciousness with every bite.

Heat the oven to 375°F (190°C). Make the flax eggs by combining the flaxseed meal and water and set it aside. In a large bowl, beat the butter, nut or seed butter, vanilla and sugar with an electric mixer on medium speed, scraping the bowl occasionally, until well blended. Next, beat in the applesauce and flax eggs until well mixed. On low speed, beat in the flour, baking soda, baking powder and salt.

Dust a piece of parchment paper with flour and turn the cookie dough out onto the parchment paper. With floured hands, press the cookie dough out into a 9 x 12-inch (23 x 30-cm) rectangle, just as you would when making cinnamon rolls.

Next, make the cinnamon sugar filling. In a medium bowl, stir together the sugar, cinnamon and salt, then using a fork or your hands, add in the oil and stir until the mixture is a wet, spreadable crumble. Spread the filling over the cookie dough, getting as close to the edges as possible. Roll the dough over the filling along the long edge, just as if you are rolling cinnamon rolls. If the dough is too sticky to roll with your hands, use the parchment paper to help you roll the dough into a log. With a sharp, floured knife, slice the log as you would cinnamon rolls into 1-inch (2.5-cm) slices, then place each cookie on ungreased cookie sheets. Mold the cookies into circles with your hands and then bake for 10 to 12 minutes. Allow them to cool for 15 to 20 minutes before frosting.

To make the cream cheese frosting, beat the butter and cream cheese together until smooth and then add in the sugar a little at a time until the frosting forms. Frost the cookies and sprinkle with more cinnamon, if desired.

YIELD: *14 large cookies*

2 tbsp (14 g) flaxseed meal

5 tbsp (75 ml) water

½ cup (108 g) vegan butter

¼ cup (63 g) nut or seed butter

1 tsp pure vanilla extract

½ cup (65 g) date or coconut sugar

½ cup (122 g) unsweetened applesauce

2 cups (296 g) gluten-free all-purpose baking flour, plus more for dusting

1 tsp baking soda

1 tsp baking powder

Pinch of salt

CINNAMON SUGAR FILLING

1 cup (130 g) date or coconut sugar

2 tbsp (16 g) cinnamon, plus more for sprinkling (optional)

Pinch of salt

5 tbsp (75 g) coconut oil, melted

CREAM CHEESE FROSTING

½ cup (108 g) vegan butter, softened

½ cup (120 g) vegan cream cheese

2 cups (240 g) confectioners' sugar

CLASSIC CHOCOLATE CAKE

A classic chocolate cake with a gluten-free, vegan makeover and some sneaky ingredients to make it moist and healthy-ish. You can choose to completely frost this cake or you can simply leave the cake naked and add a middle and top layer of chocolate buttercream frosting. I like to serve this chocolate cake with fresh berries, but it's totally delish on its own.

Preheat the oven to 350°F (175°C). Grease two 9-inch (23-cm) round cake pans. To make the flax eggs, combine the flaxseed meal and water in a small bowl and set it aside. In a large bowl, whisk together the flour, tapioca starch, cocoa powder, baking soda, baking powder and salt. In a separate bowl, combine the bananas, avocado, milk, vanilla, maple syrup and flax eggs. In a microwave-safe bowl, melt the chocolate chips with the oil for 45 seconds to 1 minute, then add it to the other wet ingredients. Pour the wet ingredients into the dry and stir to combine. Don't overmix. Pour the batter into the two prepared round cake pans and bake for 20 to 25 minutes, until a toothpick inserted into it comes out clean and the top of the cake looks done. The edges will start to look crispy and the cake will be slightly firm to the touch.

To make the frosting, beat the butter and vanilla together until smooth, then add the sugar a little bit at a time until the frosting forms. Allow the chocolate cake to cool completely before frosting. Garnish with fresh berries, if desired. Store covered on your counter for up to 3 days.

NOTE: *You may also use a 9 x 13–inch (23 x 33–cm) cake pan; the cake will just be thinner.*

YIELD: *2 (9-inch [23-cm]) round cakes*

CAKE

4 tbsp (28 g) flaxseed meal

⅔ cup (160 ml) water

2 cups (296 g) gluten-free baking flour

½ cup (65 g) tapioca starch

½ cup (48 g) unsweetened cocoa powder

2 tsp (9 g) baking soda

2 tsp (9 g) baking powder

½ tsp salt

2 large bananas, ripe and smashed with a fork

1 large avocado, peeled, pitted and mashed

1¾ cups (420 ml) plant milk

1 tsp pure vanilla extract

1 cup (240 ml) maple syrup

1 cup (168 g) dark chocolate chips

2 tbsp (30 ml) coconut oil, melted

CHOCOLATE BUTTERCREAM FROSTING

1 cup (215 g) vegan butter

1 tsp pure vanilla extract

4 cups (480 g) confectioners' sugar

TOPPING (OPTIONAL)

Fresh berries

GRAIN-FREE
BLUEBERRY SCONES

I always thought of scones as more of a breakfast item, but sometimes I think they are too sweet to eat for breakfast, so these blueberry scones make the perfect dessert that just so happens to double as breakfast, if you so choose. They are made grain-free using cassava flour and are so soft with just the right amount of crispiness on the outside. Drizzle them with easy homemade blueberry glaze for extra blueberry flavor and to kick them up to full-on dessert!

In a small bowl, combine the flaxseed meal and water to make the flax eggs and set it aside. In another small bowl or glass measuring cup, combine the milk, apple cider vinegar and vanilla and let it sit to form a vegan "buttermilk."

Preheat the oven to 350°F (175°C). Line a baking sheet with parchment paper. In a large bowl, whisk together the flour, sugar, salt, baking powder and cardamom. Using a pastry blender or your hands, cut in the butter until the mixture is crumbly.

Add the flax eggs, milk mixture and blueberries to the dry ingredients and stir until a moist batter forms. The mixture should be well combined and hold together in a ball.

On the prepared baking sheet, press the dough into an 8-inch (20-cm) circle, about ¾ inch (2 cm) thick. Brush the top with additional milk and sprinkle with a touch of confectioners' sugar, if desired. Using a sharp knife, cut the circle into eight pie slice–shaped wedges. Separate the wedges from each other and then bake them for 35 to 40 minutes until they look golden brown. Remove from the oven and cool.

To make the glaze, combine the blueberries and milk in a blender or food processer and blend until smooth. Pour the blueberry-milk mixture into a medium bowl, then add the sugar. Stir to combine and then drizzle over the scones and serve. Store leftover scones uncovered on your counter for up to 3 days.

YIELD: *8 scones*

SCONES

4 tbsp (28 g) flaxseed meal

⅔ cup (160 ml) water

⅓ cup (80 ml) plant milk, plus more for brushing

1 tsp apple cider vinegar

1 tsp pure vanilla extract

2 cups (244 g) cassava flour

⅓ cup (43 g) coconut sugar

½ tsp salt

1 tbsp (14 g) baking powder

¼ tsp cardamom

½ cup (108 g) vegan butter, cold

6 oz (170 g) blueberries, fresh or frozen

Confectioners' sugar, for sprinkling

BLUEBERRY GLAZE (OPTIONAL)

¼ cup (37 g) blueberries

3 tbsp (45 ml) plant milk

1 cup (120 g) confectioners' sugar

Easy
EGG SWAPS

Replacing eggs was a tricky one to learn. Eggs help baked goods rise, they bind ingredients and they add moisture, which keeps your desserts fluffy. But the good news is, there are lots of egg replacements out there, and I'm going to talk about some of my faves!

Aquafaba

Have you heard of this trendy new discovery? Aquafaba is the brine from a can of unsalted chickpeas. (Salted brine doesn't work!) This is one of my favorite baking secrets! Because it's full of starch from the chickpeas, it makes a great egg replacement binder in baked goods. And unlike some of the other egg replacements, it actually creates lift in recipes, much like eggs. When whipped on high with a stand or hand mixer for 5 to 10 minutes, it fluffs up just like whipped egg whites! It's perfect for meringue and macarons, but you can also use it unwhipped in your cookies, cakes, breads, brownies, etc. I suggest lightly whisking the aquafaba to aerate it before adding it. Although it has a *slight* chickpea flavor on its own, when combined with sugar or added to your batter, it's nearly flavorless when baked.

3 tablespoons (45 ml) aquafaba = 1 whole egg

2 tablespoons (30 ml) aquafaba = 1 egg white

1 tablespoon (15 ml) aquafaba = 1 egg yolk

Flax Eggs

This is one of my favorite go-to egg replacements. Using flax eggs in your baking acts as a binder, helping the structure of baked goods much like eggs do, and adds a little fluffiness. If you've never used a flax egg before, you simply soak ground flaxseed meal in water and let it sit for about 5 minutes until it gels up and is similar to an egg in consistency. Be sure to use ground flaxseed meal and not whole flaxseeds. I have also found that using double the amount of flax eggs compared to real eggs works best. For example, if a recipe calls for 2 eggs, it's best to double that and use 4 flax eggs.

1 tablespoon (7 g) flaxseed meal + 3 tablespoons (45 ml) of water = approximately 1 egg. Let it soak until it becomes gelatinous.

Agar Agar Powder

Agar agar powder is derived from seaweed or algae and is commonly used in vegan desserts to thicken them or create a gelatin- or custard-like texture. Agar agar powder is a great gelatin replacement, but it's also a great egg replacement, especially when a recipe calls for egg whites. It's flavorless too. It can be used in your baked goods as a binder, much like eggs would act, but it won't necessarily allow the recipe to rise like eggs would, so combining it with baking powder or even a mashed banana helps to keep the dessert from being too dense without the eggs.

1 tablespoon (24 g) agar agar powder + 1 tablespoon (15 ml) water = approximately 1 egg. Use 2 tablespoons (48 g) agar agar powder with 2 tablespoons (30 ml) water for a stiffer texture.

Unsweetened Applesauce

Applesauce adds moisture, but too much can keep your bakery soggy and even rubbery. I don't use this quite as often as the rest, but it is a good option. It's best used in muffins, brownies and cakes.

¼ cup (61 g) applesauce = 1 egg

Nut or Seed Butter

Using nut or seed butter such as peanut butter, almond butter, cashew butter or sunflower seed butter adds texture, lightness and moisture. It doesn't make your baked goods rise, but this is one of my favorite replacements to keep my baked goods moist. Be sure to use creamy nut or seed butters and not crunchy. Your baked goods may result in a nuttier or seedier flavor, so it's best used in brownies, pan cakes, cookies and certain cake flavors. Using one of these may also make your batter a bit darker, so if you're going for a lighter-colored dessert, opt for one of the other replacements instead.

3 tablespoons (48 g) nut or seed butter = 1 egg. I usually add at least ¼ cup (64 g) because it makes the final product more moist and flavorful.

Avocado, Banana or Pumpkin, Oh My!

Using one of these nutrient-dense foods not only adds moisture but also a bit of sweetness as well. Always mash your avocado and banana before adding, and be sure to use only pure pumpkin puree and not canned pumpkin pie. Also try using very ripe bananas, ones about to go bad, as they are mushier and sweeter.

¼ cup (38 g) mashed avocado, (38 g) banana or (61 g) pumpkin = 1 egg

Chia Seeds

Similar to flax eggs, chia eggs are made with chia seeds. Again, you simply soak the chia seeds in water and let it sit for about 5 minutes until it gels up and is similar to an egg in consistency. Chia can act as a binder, and it also gets gelatinous like the flaxseed meal. Unlike the flaxseed meal, chia eggs have a less nutty or earthy flavor, so they don't offer much added taste, making them a great choice.

1 tablespoon (10 g) chia seeds + 2½ tablespoons (38 ml) water = 1 egg

Dairy-Free Unsweetened Yogurt

Using dairy-free yogurt adds creaminess and moisture, but be sure to read the yogurt labels as many store-bought brands contain a lot of sugar, so be mindful of that if you're trying to keep your dessert low sugar. This replacement works best in muffins and cakes but can make your batter too heavy if too much is added. Try beating it before adding to make it fluffier.

¼ cup (60 ml) yogurt = 1 egg

Vinegar & Baking Soda

Using baking soda is not new for baking; we use it often in traditional baking to help baked goods rise and become fluffier. But vinegar also helps baked goods rise and become fluffier, and contrary to what you might think, it doesn't give your baked goods a vinegary taste. Combining vinegar and plant milk (dairy-free milk) and letting it sit creates a vegan buttermilk that actually curdles to replace traditional buttermilk in baking too.

1 teaspoon baking soda + 1 tablespoon (15 ml) vinegar = 1 egg

It almost seemed impossible to enjoy the following recipes without eggs, so I chose the recipes in this chapter to prove that you can, indeed, omit the eggs and still have a scrumptious treat! My Vegan Marshmallows (page 101) have gone viral and for good reason, so of course I want you to have this recipe right at your fingertips. And the others in this section are just as surprising considering that there are no eggs involved . . . you'll see!

CINNAMON SUGAR
CRÈME BRÛLÉE

Did you think that crème brûlée was off the menu?! Well, I'm so excited to bring you a very similar, just-as-creamy vegan version of this popular European dessert recipe—without the cream or the eggs! Perfect for date night, you won't believe how simple this crème brûlée is to make, and you'll definitely be impressing your guests with this fourth-course dish.

Preheat the oven to 325°F (160°C). Place crème brûlée dishes or ramekins into a large cake pan or roasting pan. In a medium saucepan, heat the solid coconut milk, vanilla, salt, arrowroot powder, cinnamon and maple syrup over medium heat until the mixture thickens and is smooth and creamy. If it's not completely smooth, transfer the mixture to a blender and blend until smooth. Evenly distribute the mixture into the crème brûlée dishes or ramekins. Heat the water in the microwave until almost boiling, then very carefully pour enough hot water into the pan to come halfway up the outsides of the ramekins, being very careful not to splash water into the ramekins.

Bake the crème brûlée for 20 minutes. When the ramekins are cool enough to touch, transfer them to a cooling rack to cool completely for about 1 hour. Cover the ramekins with plastic wrap and place them in the fridge overnight.

Remove the crème brûlée from the refrigerator, divide the cane sugar equally among the ramekins and spread it evenly on top. Using a torch, melt the sugar to form a crispy top. If you don't have a torch, you may place the ramekins in the oven and broil them, watching very carefully so they don't burn.

NOTE: *Propane gas torches are highly flammable and should be kept away from heat, open flame and prolonged exposure to sunlight. They should be used only in well-ventilated areas. Follow the torch manufacturer's instructions for use.*

YIELD: *2–4 servings*

CRÈME BRÛLÉE
1 (13.5-oz [400-ml]) can coconut milk, solid part only
2 tsp (10 ml) pure vanilla extract
⅛ tsp salt
3 tbsp (24 g) arrowroot powder
¼ tsp cinnamon
¼ cup (60 ml) maple syrup
2 cups (480 ml) water

TOPPING
2 tbsp (12 g) cane sugar

VEGAN MARSHMALLOWS

If you thought marshmallows were completely off the table in a vegan lifestyle, think again! Allow me to introduce you to the easiest homemade vegan marshmallow recipe! These gluten-free, vegan marshmallows are made with only six ingredients, so they couldn't be simpler. If you've never whipped up aquafaba, you're in for a real magical surprise! Try toasting these marshmallows with a kitchen torch or lighter for that campfire vibe.

First, line an 8 x 8–inch (20 x 20–cm) baking pan with parchment paper, then spray with coconut oil and generously dust with tapioca starch or arrowroot powder. Set aside.

In your stand mixer, beat the aquafaba on high for 10 to 15 minutes. Alternatively, you can do this with a hand mixer.

Add the tapioca syrup to a small saucepan and bring to a boil. While waiting for it to boil, dissolve the agar agar in the water, then add it to the saucepan.

Whisk the syrup continuously until it reaches a rolling boil, then add the salt and vanilla to the saucepan. Whisk to combine, then remove from the heat.

Turn your mixer down to low and slowly pour the syrup mixture into the aquafaba to create a marshmallow fluff. Quickly pour the fluff into the prepared baking pan, smooth the surface and let it rest at room temperature for about 3 hours or overnight, or if using it as marshmallow fluff, use it immediately, as it starts to set up very quickly.

Once it has set up, dust with tapioca starch or arrowroot powder and turn it out on a tapioca starch–dusted surface and slice into squares (or desired shape). Store in an airtight container. These marshmallows are best when consumed the same day or within 2 days.

YIELD: *9–12 square marshmallows*

2 to 3 tbsp (16 to 24 g) tapioca starch or arrowroot powder, for dusting

½ cup (120 ml) aquafaba

1 cup (240 ml) tapioca syrup (see Note)

2 tbsp (16 g) agar agar powder

6 tbsp (90 ml) water

¼ tsp salt

2 tsp (10 ml) pure vanilla extract

NOTE: *Using tapioca syrup allows this recipe to be a lower-sugar, grain-free option, but you may also use regular corn syrup. If you desire a sweeter marshmallow, you can dust them with a little confectioners' sugar.*

LEMON CUSTARD
GRANOLA TARTLETS

This healthy-ish dessert can easily double as breakfast with its granola- and pretzel-based crust and light and airy lemon custard filling. With just a hint of lemon, this dainty, pretty dessert will be a hit at your next summer brunch served with fresh berries and a dollop of coconut whipped cream.

Preheat the oven to 350°F (175°C). To make the crust, in a food processor, pulse the granola and pretzels into semi-fine crumbs. Add the butter, tapioca or brown rice syrup and cinnamon, and pulse until the mixture holds together when pinched. Press the dough into two 5-inch (13-cm) greased tartlet pans. Bake the crust until toasted, about 8 minutes, remove and then gently press the crust down with the back of a spoon to make the well deeper for the filling.

In a medium saucepan, heat the milk, lemon juice, vanilla, salt, arrowroot powder, maple syrup and lemon zest over medium heat until the mixture thickens and is smooth and creamy, 8 to 10 minutes. Pour the filling into the crusts and allow them to fully cool to room temperature, then transfer them to the fridge to set up for about 4 hours.

Serve with coconut whipped cream and fresh berries, if desired.

YIELD: *2 (5-inch [13-cm]) tartlets*

CRUST
1 cup (103 g) gluten-free granola
1 cup (120 g) gluten-free pretzels
¼ cup (54 g) vegan butter
2 tbsp (30 ml) tapioca syrup or brown rice syrup
Pinch of cinnamon

FILLING
¾ cup (180 ml) coconut milk
1 tbsp (15 ml) lemon juice
2 tsp (10 ml) pure vanilla extract
⅛ tsp salt
3 tbsp (24 g) arrowroot powder
¼ cup (60 ml) maple syrup
1 lemon, zested

TOPPINGS (OPTIONAL)
Fluffy Coconut Whipped Cream (page 154)
Fresh berries

DECADENT
CHOCOLATE MOUSSE

This rich and creamy chocolate mousse is the perfect dessert when you have company over. It's such a simple recipe to make. You only need about ten minutes to prepare it, then you leave it in the fridge overnight to set up, which means you can make it the day before then simply top it with fresh berries, chocolate shavings or even coconut whipped cream, if your heart so desires.

Heat the coconut milk, dark chocolate, maple syrup, oil and salt in a saucepan until the chocolate is melted and the mixture is simmering, but not boiling, whisking frequently until glossy.

Remove the chocolate mixture from the heat and allow it to cool for 10 to 15 minutes, then pour into glasses, pudding cups, bowls or ramekins and place them in the fridge overnight to set up. Serve with fresh berries, chocolate shavings or even coconut whipped cream, if desired.

YIELD: *6–8 servings*

CHOCOLATE MOUSSE
1 (13.5-oz [400-ml]) can coconut milk

8 oz (226 g) dark chocolate

¼ cup (60 ml) maple syrup

¼ cup (60 g) coconut oil

½ tsp salt

TOPPINGS (OPTIONAL)
Fresh berries

Chocolate shavings

Fluffy Coconut Whipped Cream (page 154)

PECAN PIE
COOKIE CUPS

When you want the flavor of pecan pie but the simplicity of making cookies, you combine them into one fabulous dessert recipe! The cookie cup crust, which I developed in collaboration with Natalie from Feasting on Fruit, is filled with a naturally sweetened, egg-free and corn syrup–free filling, garnished with chopped pecans and then baked for 25 minutes. Be sure to allow these cookie cups to cool completely before trying to remove them from the muffin tin, then dig in!

Preheat your oven to 350°F (175°C). In a food processor, grind the granola until you achieve a fine texture, then add in the baking soda, cinnamon, flour and salt and pulse to combine.

Place the crust mixture into a medium bowl, then stir in the almond butter, maple syrup and vanilla until you have a cookie dough–like consistency.

Spray a large muffin tin with coconut oil, then gently press the dough into the muffin tin cups equally, making a well in the middle of each with your fingers. Set aside.

To make the pecan pie filling, add the pecans, butter, maple syrup, sugar, tapioca starch, cinnamon, vanilla and salt to your blender and blend until very smooth and creamy. Spoon the filling into each cookie cup almost to the top, but make sure to leave room for chopped pecans. Garnish each cookie cup with chopped pecans and bake in the oven for 25 minutes. Cool completely before removing from the muffin tin and serve!

YIELD: *8 large cookie cups*

COOKIE CUP CRUST

2 cups (206 g) plain gluten-free granola

1 tsp baking soda

½ tsp cinnamon

½ cup (61 g) cassava flour

Pinch of salt

½ cup (125 g) unsweetened almond butter

½ cup (120 ml) maple syrup

1 tsp pure vanilla extract

PECAN PIE FILLING

1 cup (109 g) chopped pecans

¼ cup (54 g) vegan butter

½ cup (120 ml) maple syrup

½ cup (65 g) coconut sugar

¼ cup (33 g) tapioca starch

1 tsp cinnamon

1 tsp pure vanilla extract

¼ tsp salt

TOPPING

½ cup (55 g) chopped pecans

CUSTARD
BREAD PUDDING

With notes of a French toast casserole, this bread pudding is made by soaking gluten-free bread in a maple cinnamon, custard-like mixture overnight, then baking it in the oven with a cinnamon sugar streusel topping for the ultimate comforting dessert.

Add the bread to an 8 x 8–inch (20 x 20–cm) square or 9-inch (23-cm) round baking dish.

In a medium saucepan, heat the milk, vanilla, salt, arrowroot powder, cinnamon and maple syrup over medium heat until the mixture thickens and is smooth and creamy. If it's not completely smooth, transfer the mixture to a blender and blend until smooth. Pour the coconut mixture over the bread and toss the bread around with a spoon to make sure all of the bread is soaking in the mixture. Cover and refrigerate overnight.

The next day, preheat the oven to 350°F (175°C). To make the crumble topping, in a large bowl, combine the flour, sugar, cinnamon and salt. Add the butter and cut into the dry mixture until it forms a streusel-like texture. Crumble the streusel evenly over top of the bread pudding and bake in the oven for 35 to 40 minutes.

Allow the bread pudding to cool slightly and serve with No-Churn Vanilla Ice Cream, if desired.

YIELD: *4–6 servings*

BREAD PUDDING

4 cups (544 g) gluten-free bread, cubed

1 (13.5-oz [400-ml]) can coconut milk

2 tsp (10 ml) pure vanilla extract

⅛ tsp salt

3 tbsp (24 g) arrowroot powder

½ tsp cinnamon

½ cup (120 ml) maple syrup

CRUMBLE TOPPING

¾ cup (111 g) gluten-free flour of choice

¼ cup (33 g) coconut or date sugar

2 tsp (5 g) cinnamon

¼ tsp salt

¼ cup (54 g) vegan butter

TOPPING (OPTIONAL)

No-Churn Vanilla Ice Cream (page 153)

SOFT CHOCOLATE CREAM SANDWICH COOKIES

Move over Oreo cookies, there's a new, healthier chocolate cream sandwich cookie in town! It's really embarrassing how many Oreos I used to eat in one sitting, and they were always dunked in milk because I am definitely more of a soft cookie fan. So with this recipe, we're skipping the milk and going straight to soft and pillowy cookies, and hopefully, these make you forget all about their popular counterpart.

Preheat the oven to 375°F (190°C). Make the flax eggs by combining the flaxseed meal and water in a small bowl and set it aside. In a large bowl, whisk together the flour, tapioca starch, baking soda, baking powder, cocoa powder and salt and set aside.

In a separate large bowl, beat the butter, sugar, nut or seed butter and vanilla with an electric mixer on medium speed, scraping the bowl occasionally, until well blended. Then, beat in the pumpkin puree and flax eggs until well mixed. On low speed, beat in the flour mixture until well combined.

Lay out macaron baking mats (if using) onto baking sheets. You'll need two baking mats, but you can also eyeball your cookies instead—just note you may have fewer cookie sandwiches depending on their size. Scoop 1 tablespoon (15 g) of cookie batter and roll it into a ball with your hands. Place on the baking mats or sheets and lightly flatten the ball into a disc shape, making sure it isn't too thin. Repeat for all of the batter, then bake for 10 to 12 minutes. Let them cool while you make the cream filling.

In a large bowl using an electric mixer, beat the shortening, butter and vanilla until smooth, then slowly add the sugar and beat until the filling is sturdy.

Pipe or spread the bottom of half the cookies with filling and place another cookie, bottom side down, on top. Keep them stored in an airtight container on your counter for up to 3 days.

YIELD: *16 small cookie sandwiches*

CHOCOLATE COOKIES

2 tbsp (14 g) flaxseed meal

5 tbsp (75 ml) water

1 cup (112 g) coconut flour

½ cup (65 g) tapioca starch

1 tsp baking soda

1 tsp baking powder

½ cup (48 g) unsweetened cocoa powder

Pinch of salt

1 cup (215 g) vegan butter

1 cup (130 g) coconut sugar

¼ cup (63 g) nut or seed butter

1 tsp pure vanilla extract

½ cup (123 g) pure pumpkin puree

CREAM FILLING

½ cup (103 g) vegan shortening

½ cup (108 g) vegan butter, softened

½ tsp pure vanilla extract

2 cups (240 g) confectioners' sugar

GRAIN-FREE LEMON BARS

These lemon bars are a tad different than most cakey lemon bars you might have had, but they've still got the same great zesty taste! The lemon filling is extra thick and just a tad creamy and sits on an irresistible shortbread crust. Bake these bars at a bit of a lower temperature to avoid overbaking. Dust with confectioners' sugar for an extra-sweet treat.

Preheat the oven to 325°F (160°C). Line an 8 x 8–inch (20 x 20–cm) baking pan with parchment paper and set aside. Alternatively, you can use a rectangular baking pan if you like thinner lemon bars.

In a large bowl, whisk together the flours, sugar and salt, then add the oil and vanilla. Stir to combine. Press the crust into the baking pan and bake for 8 minutes.

Remove the crust and let it cool while you prepare the filling, but keep the oven on. Add the solid coconut milk, lemon juice, lemon zest, banana, vanilla, maple syrup, oil, flour, tapioca starch and turmeric (if using) to a blender and blend until smooth. Pour over the crust and place it back into the oven for 20 minutes, until the center is not jiggly. Chill the lemon bars for 2 hours in the fridge or overnight. Before serving, dust with confectioners' sugar, if desired.

YIELD: *6–8 bars*

SHORTBREAD CRUST

1 cup (122 g) cassava flour

¼ cup (24 g) almond flour

¼ cup (28 g) coconut flour

3 tbsp (24 g) coconut sugar

Pinch of salt

½ cup (120 g) coconut oil, softened

1 tsp pure vanilla extract

FILLING

½ cup (120 g) coconut milk, solid part only

⅔ cup (160 ml) lemon juice (about 4 lemons)

1 tbsp (6 g) lemon zest

1 medium banana

1 tsp pure vanilla extract

½ cup (120 ml) maple syrup

1 tbsp (14 g) coconut oil, melted

2 tbsp (16 g) cassava flour

2 tbsp (16 g) tapioca starch

Pinch of turmeric, for color (optional)

TOPPING (OPTIONAL)

Confectioners' sugar

No Oven Needed!
(NO-BAKE TREATS)

I've never met anyone who doesn't love dessert! So, here's the thing: My sweet tooth sometimes gets the better of me, but when I'm indulging smarter, I certainly don't feel as bad—both mentally and physically. Now, we all know that eating more fruits and vegetables is important; that doesn't mean we necessarily do it, but we at least have the knowledge that raw fruits and veggies are good for us. Raw, no-bake desserts have that same principle, not that I am saying desserts are always good for us. However, uncooked foods retain way more nutritional value than cooked foods. When you include things like raw nuts in your desserts, for example, you're offering your body the highest possible form of vitamins and minerals these nuts have to offer.

Raw foods digest quicker, providing less opportunity for indigestion, gas and bloating to set in. They also help to maintain a healthy acidic level within our digestive system to keep your immune system in working order, helping you to fight off infection faster and better. It's true, desserts usually have carbs. It's no secret, but you know what? We *need* carbs. Sure, it's better to get your carbs from fresh produce, but sometimes that's just not as fun, you feel me? That's why, when using whole foods—like nuts, plant flours, natural sugars, raw cacao powder, etc.—I feel much better about my carb intake and allowing myself to indulge. There is no oven time required for no-bake desserts, making these recipes very appealing because, generally, they are easier to make.

Traditional no-bake desserts are just that—no bake. But they might still require some heating to melt ingredients, like chocolate or coconut oil—so I don't call them completely raw desserts. That being said, because you can often melt ingredients over low heat as opposed to baked goods that are heated for half an hour, or sometimes longer, you can still retain some of that nutritional value. And why yes, pure chocolate (with no added junk) does in fact have some health benefits! You can even sneak in some superfood powders, like matcha and pink pitaya powder, to not only make these no-bake desserts taste fantastic but look the part too!

I wanted to include a no-bake chapter because they are some of my favorite desserts to make and to eat! The following recipes are so simple they needed to have a place in this book.

NO-BAKE PEANUT BUTTER CUP BARS

Now you can enjoy peanut butter cups in bar form! These bars have a raw chocolate cookie dough crust, a creamy peanut butter filling and a top layer of melted chocolate that's garnished with chopped peanut butter cups. These No-Bake Peanut Butter Cup Bars are also naturally sweetened!

Line an 8 x 8–inch (20 x 20–cm) baking pan with parchment paper. To make the crust, whisk together the flour, cocoa powder and salt in a large bowl, then add the peanut butter, vanilla, maple syrup and chocolate chips. Stir everything together until a dough forms, then press your cookie dough into the prepared baking pan and set aside.

To make the filling, in a large saucepan over medium heat, melt the peanut butter, butter, maple syrup, flour, oil, milk, vanilla and salt, whisking continuously until almost boiling. Remove from the heat and pour it over the cookie dough crust. Place in the freezer uncovered for 1 hour.

To make the chocolate topping, melt the chocolate chips together with the oil in a glass container in the microwave for 30 seconds. Remove, stir and, if needed, place back into the microwave for 10-second increments.

Remove the pan from the freezer and pour the melted chocolate over the top. Sprinkle the chopped peanut butter cups over the top and stick it back into the freezer until set, at least 4 hours, preferably overnight.

Store the bars in the fridge or freezer. If you store the bars in the freezer, allow the bars to thaw for 15 to 20 minutes before enjoying.

YIELD: *9 large bars*

COOKIE DOUGH CRUST

2 cups (192 g) almond flour

¼ cup (24 g) unsweetened cocoa powder

Pinch of salt

6 tbsp (96 g) peanut butter

1 tsp pure vanilla extract

¼ cup (60 ml) maple syrup

6 tbsp (66 g) dark chocolate chips

PEANUT BUTTER FILLING

1 cup (258 g) peanut butter

½ cup (108 g) vegan butter (or coconut butter)

3 tbsp (45 ml) maple syrup

⅓ cup (32 g) blanched almond flour

2 tbsp (30 g) coconut oil

1 (13.5-oz [400-ml]) can coconut milk

1 tsp pure vanilla extract

¼ tsp salt

CHOCOLATE TOPPING

1 cup (168 g) dark chocolate chips

4 tbsp (60 g) coconut oil

TOPPING

3 oz (85 g) dark chocolate peanut butter cups, roughly chopped

AVOCADO CHOCOLATE PIE

As one of the sneakily healthier dessert options in this book, you'll never believe the star in this pie is avocado! Avocado and chocolate together are a creamy dream team that will leave you surprised after every bite. The simple peanut crust is made with just three ingredients, the chocolate avocado filling is made with only five ingredients and there's no baking required, which could possibly move this pie up on your list of favorites.

To make the crust, in a food processor, pulse the peanuts and sugar into semi-fine crumbs. Add the oil and pulse until the mixture holds together when pinched and starts to look like dough. Press the dough into a greased 9-inch (23-cm) pie pan and set aside.

To make the filling, scoop the flesh of the avocados into a blender along with the cocoa powder, maple syrup, oil and vanilla and blend until smooth. Pour the filling over the crust and chill in the fridge for 4 hours or until firm, preferably overnight. Sprinkle with sea salt before serving, if desired. Store leftover slices in an airtight container in the fridge for a couple of days.

YIELD: *1 (9-inch [23-cm]) pie*

CRUST

2 cups (292 g) peanuts, roasted and salted

¾ cup (98 g) coconut sugar

½ cup (120 g) coconut oil, melted

FILLING

3 medium avocados

½ cup (48 g) unsweetened cocoa powder

½ cup (120 ml) maple syrup

⅓ cup (80 g) coconut oil, melted

2 tsp (10 ml) pure vanilla extract

TOPPING (OPTIONAL)

Sea salt

CHIA PUDDING

Pudding gets a healthy boost that can make this dessert double as a quick and easy breakfast too! Chia seeds are packed with fiber and are among the best plant-based sources of omega-3 fatty acids. They're also loaded with quality protein. I guess it's true what they say: Good things do come in tiny packages. This chia pudding ditches the dairy but sure doesn't ditch its rich and creamy texture. Only five ingredients are needed to make this pudding and the topping options are limitless!

Stir or blend the chia seeds, milk, maple syrup, vanilla and salt together and re-stir every few minutes until the pudding starts to thicken. The seeds will sink to the bottom unless you keep stirring. Once it starts to thicken, pour into glasses and chill. This may be made the night before and chilled overnight. Top with your desired toppings, maybe even a scoop of ice cream or a dollop of coconut whipped cream!

YIELD: *2 servings*

PUDDING
¼ cup (41 g) chia seeds
1 cup (240 ml) plant milk
2 tbsp (30 ml) maple syrup
1 tsp pure vanilla extract
Pinch of salt

TOPPINGS
Fresh berries
Vegan Caramel Sauce (page 157)
Chocolate Ganache (page 158) or chocolate chips
Sautéed cinnamon apples
Caramelized bananas
Ice cream
Fluffy Coconut Whipped Cream (page 154)

COCONUT
PEPPERMINT PATTIES

Making your own candy has never been easier (or healthier!). These copycat New York peppermint patties are bursting with flavor and certainly live up to the store-bought alternative. I like to make a batch and keep these delicious little minty treats in my fridge or freezer for a quick, sweet snack.

Line a baking sheet with parchment paper. In a food processor or blender, blend the shredded coconut, flour and salt together until smooth. Add the solid coconut cream, sugar and peppermint extract and blend again until a batter forms. You want the batter to easily stick together and not crumble. If it's too dry, add 1 teaspoon of water at a time until you are able to roll the batter into a ball.

Scoop about a spoonful at a time and, using your hands, roll the batter into balls, then place them onto the prepared baking sheet. Flatten them into thick rounds, pressing the outer edges together to remain a circle. Place them into the freezer for about 1 hour.

Melt the chocolate chips and oil together in a bowl in the microwave, about 45 to 60 seconds. Remove the coconut patties from the freezer and, using a fork, gently dip each one into the melted chocolate until they are fully covered. Let the excess chocolate run off and then gently place each one back onto the prepared baking sheet. Refrigerate until the chocolate is set, about 30 minutes. Keep them stored in the fridge or freezer.

YIELD: *16 patties*

1 cup (93 g) unsweetened shredded coconut

1 cup (112 g) coconut flour

Pinch of salt

1 (13.5-oz [400-ml]) can coconut cream

4 tbsp (32 g) confectioners' sugar (may substitute with maple or agave syrup)

1 tbsp (15 ml) pure peppermint extract

1 cup (168 g) dark chocolate chips

1 tbsp (15 g) coconut oil

EDIBLE CHOCOLATE CHIP COOKIE DOUGH

Any other cookie dough lovers out there? I often find myself snacking on the cookie dough, sometimes more than actually wanting fully baked cookies. . . . Are you with me? Well, if that sounds familiar, this cookie dough is for you! It's safe to eat raw and made with ingredients like almond flour, maple syrup and peanut butter, so it's actually pretty healthy. If you eat the whole dang batch, you don't have to feel bad! At least that's what I tell myself. I think you'll love keeping this sweet snack stashed in your fridge for when the cookie (dough) craving hits.

In a food processor, blend together the flour, salt, peanut butter, vanilla and maple or agave syrup until a dough forms. Transfer the dough to a medium bowl and fold in the chocolate chips. Alternatively, you can stir together all of the ingredients in a large mixing bowl until a dough forms. Roll into balls for little cookie dough bites or dig in with a spoon! Store in an airtight container in your fridge for up to 3 days.

YIELD: *2–4 servings*

1½ cups (144 g) almond flour

¼ tsp salt

¼ cup (65 g) peanut butter (or other nut or seed butter)

1 tsp pure vanilla extract

¼ cup (60 ml) maple or agave syrup

¼ cup (42 g) dark chocolate chips

NO-BAKE MINI
KEY LIME PIES

A classic sweet and tangy pie made mini! Summer's favorite creamy citrus pie just got a whole lot cuter and a whole lot easier to make. If you can't find key limes, you can definitely use regular limes, and it might actually be easier, as they yield more juice with minimal flavor difference! Not to mention regular limes can typically be found all year round, taking this dessert recipe to a multi-seasonal indulgence.

Line a muffin tin with paper liners. To make the crust, in a large bowl, whisk together the flours and salt, then stir in the vanilla, maple syrup, peanut butter, oil or butter and water. Press the crust into the muffin tins, then pack the crust down using the back of a spoon. You'll want to fill each cup about half full with crust. Set aside.

To make the filling, drain and rinse the cashews, then add them to a blender or food processor with the lime juice, lime zest, solid coconut cream, butter or oil, salt, maple or agave syrup and vanilla. Blend until smooth and creamy. Pour the filling evenly over top of the crusts, then place the muffin tin in the refrigerator overnight to set up. Serve with coconut whipped cream, if desired. Store in the fridge for up to 3 days or you may freeze them. If you freeze them, let them thaw at room temperature before enjoying.

NOTE: *For a more traditional texture, you can bake the crust before if you wish for about 8 to 10 minutes at 350°F (175°C), then add the filling and refrigerate overnight.*

YIELD: *6 muffin-sized pies*

CRUST
1 cup (120 g) banana flour

½ cup (60 g) oat flour

Pinch of salt

1 tsp pure vanilla extract

⅓ cup (80 ml) maple syrup

½ cup (129 g) peanut butter (or another nut or seed butter)

¼ cup (60 g) coconut oil or vegan butter, melted

¼ cup (60 ml) water

FILLING
1½ cups (219 g) raw cashews, soaked overnight or boiled for 15 minutes

¼ cup (60 ml) lime juice

1 to 2 tsp (2 to 4 g) lime zest

3 tbsp (45 g) coconut cream

¼ cup (54 g) vegan butter or coconut oil

Pinch of salt

⅓ cup (80 ml) maple or agave syrup

1 tsp pure vanilla extract

TOPPING (OPTIONAL)
Fluffy Coconut Whipped Cream (page 154)

PUMPKIN
CHEESECAKE BARS

If you're a pumpkin lover like me, it doesn't have to be fall to enjoy these Pumpkin Cheesecake Bars! This is the perfect naturally sweetened dessert to pack in some highly nutritious pumpkin all year round! These bars are made with banana flour for a gluten-free, grain-free crust filled with a no-bake vegan pumpkin cheesecake filling, then placed in the fridge to set up overnight.

Line an 8 x 8–inch (20 x 20–cm) baking pan with parchment paper. To make the crust, in a large bowl, whisk together the flour, cinnamon and salt, then stir in the sunflower seed butter, butter, vanilla, maple syrup and water. Press the crust into the baking pan, and set it aside while you make the filling.

To make the filling, add the pumpkin puree, butter, solid coconut cream, oil, maple syrup, vanilla, pumpkin pie spice, salt and cinnamon to a medium saucepan and melt it over medium heat, whisking frequently until it's smooth and creamy and has no lumps. Pour the filling over top of the crust and smooth the top with a spatula. Place it in your fridge for 4 to 6 hours, or preferably overnight, to set up.

Slice and serve the next day with dairy-free whipped cream (if desired) and sprinkled cinnamon! Store leftovers in an airtight container in the fridge for up to 4 days.

YIELD: *9–12 bars*

CRUST

2 cups (240 g) banana flour

½ tsp cinnamon

Pinch of salt

½ cup (128 g) sunflower seed butter (or another nut or seed butter)

¼ cup (54 g) vegan butter

1 tsp pure vanilla extract

⅓ cup (80 ml) maple syrup

2 tbsp (30 ml) water

PUMPKIN CHEESECAKE FILLING

1 (15-oz [425-g]) can pure pumpkin puree

½ cup (108 g) vegan butter

1 (13.5-oz [400-ml]) can coconut cream

¼ cup (60 g) coconut oil, melted

⅓ cup (80 ml) maple syrup

1 tsp pure vanilla extract

1½ tsp (3 g) pumpkin pie spice

¼ tsp salt

¼ tsp cinnamon (use ½ tsp if your pumpkin pie spice doesn't contain cinnamon)

TOPPINGS

Dairy-free whipped cream (optional)

Cinnamon

Power to
THE POWDERS

OK, so if I haven't scared you away with the different flours, egg replacements and dairy substitutes that you may or may not have heard of, let's just touch on some of the different powders that I often use in my baking recipes! I promise you'll be familiar with some of these, but maybe not all, so allow me to introduce you to the most common powders you'll find in my pantry! I'll briefly touch on what they are made from and the recipes that I most often use them in.

Baking Powder vs. Baking Soda

If you're like me and not necessarily a well-seasoned baker, then you might not know the difference between baking powder and baking soda. Admittedly, I had to look this up too. I knew that both acted as a leavening agent, but I really wasn't all too familiar with how they were used differently in baking, so I'd love to explain. Baking soda is great to use when you're making a more acidic dessert because the acid and the liquid activate the baking soda, allowing it to help make the bakery fluffier. Baking powder is a complete leavening agent, so it already contains the acidic component needed to help with rising. I definitely use baking powder more in my recipes, but if I do use baking soda, I make sure that I use an acidic ingredient like apple cider vinegar or lemon juice to help activate it. Most often, if you're unsure, I would lean toward baking powder. And you also might need more of it in gluten-free baking. I would say it's not uncommon for me to use 2 teaspoons (9 g) or even 1 tablespoon (14 g) of baking powder in some of my recipes, since you lose some of that fluffiness gluten offers.

Arrowroot Powder/Flour/Starch

From the root of a tropical plant, *Maranta arundinacea*, this herb (yes, herb) is great in baked goods and is also used for thickening sauces or fruit in desserts, like in the filling of crumb bars. It's best when added to more acidic dishes but can also be used in creamy, milk-based foods, like in small amounts for custard, as it can become slimy. You can compare it to cornstarch. Arrowroot may be whisked into the dry flour mixture or directly into the liquid part of a recipe.

Tapioca Powder/Flour/Starch

From the root of cassava, much like cassava flour, it's also used as a thickener. Tapioca can also withstand heat longer than arrowroot. Tapioca starch can also be compared to cornstarch and can either be dissolved in water prior to adding it to sauces or whisked into the dry flour mixture.

Unsweetened Cocoa Powder vs. Cacao Powder

Although very similar, there are a few differences between the two "chocolate" powders. The biggest difference is that cocoa powder is processed at much higher temperatures, fermented and roasted, thus making it lose a little bit of nutritional value. Cacao powder is also made from the fermented beans of a cacao plant, but they have not been roasted, allowing it to keep some of the vitamins and minerals as it's milled into powder. The result is a more bitter taste but higher nutritional content. The most important thing is to make sure, whether you use cocoa or cacao powder, that it's unsweetened without any added processed ingredients. Cacao is a great addition to your desserts as it's rich in antioxidants, fiber, iron and magnesium. And perhaps the very best use of the cacao bean would be in the rawest form—cacao nibs. I like to top my chocolate desserts, even smoothies, with raw cacao nibs for the highest potency of nutrients.

Psyllium Husk Powder

I didn't even know what psyllium husk was until about a year ago. Psyllium is a form of fiber harvested from the husks of the *Plantago ovata* plant. It has many health benefits in the body, but when used in baking it almost acts as gluten would—as a binder. But too much of it can make your bakery gummy, and . . . well . . . not very good. I don't use it very often, but generally, I like to stick with just 1 teaspoon of psyllium husk powder in my batter.

Agar Agar Powder

Agar agar powder, also referred to as vegan gelatin, is derived from seaweed or algae and is commonly used in vegan desserts to thicken them or create a gelatin- or custard-like dessert. Agar agar powder is flavorless too, which makes it a great replacement. It can be used in your baked goods, but also it's great used in things like homemade vegan marshmallows, puddings, panna cotta or anything you would traditionally use gelatin or Jell-O® in.

Superfood Powders

If you've visited my blog or my Instagram, you will see I am a *huge* fan of colorful foods. I love nature's candy and the rainbow of colors fresh produce comes in, but sometimes bakery can be kind of blah, being brown/orange. We use artificial food dyes to make our food look more appealing and pretty. The problem is, artificial coloring comes with a whole slew of toxic, harmful effects. Say hello to your new favorite way to color your frosting and add a pop of rainbow to your goodies: superfood powders!

So what is a "superfood powder" anyway?! It is a colorful powder made from highly nutritious foods, like pitaya (dragon fruit), that gives you a healthy boost and also happens to color your food pretty colors. It's not a new trend, as it has been around for thousands of years to use these foods to enhance your wellness, but it's definitely becoming more mainstream these days.

Pink Pitaya Powder

Pink pitaya powder is probably my favorite. Hello! It's pink! It's also very "potent," meaning you don't need a lot of it to color your food pink, and it also doesn't alter the flavor of your food like some others might. It's derived from dehydrated pink dragon fruit into a powder that can then be used in recipes as a pink food coloring! Pitaya is also high in vitamins and minerals and is nearly tasteless, so it's a great way to add a nutritious, colorful boost.

Matcha Powder

Matcha powder is another powerhouse. You might be familiar with the trendy matcha latte at your favorite coffee shops. This green, antioxidant-packed tea-based powder happens to turn your foods the most gorgeous green color while providing some really fantastic nutrients too. Matcha does contain caffeine, so if you're avoiding caffeine altogether, moringa powder is a green caffeine-free alternative.

Spirulina Powder

Spirulina powder comes in blue or green, and it's absolutely gorgeous. It is made from algae, and it does have a mild flavor if you add too much. You don't need a lot of it! Spirulina is high in so many nutrients and is actually deemed one of the most nutrient-dense foods on earth!

Turmeric Powder

Turmeric powder is probably one of the most well-known powders. You can offer your creations the most gorgeous yellow tint by using just a small amount. It does have a distinct taste, so just a little in baked goods goes a long way. Turmeric also provides some great health benefits, like helping to reduce inflammation. It's most widely used in Indian cuisine, but it is becoming more widespread for its coloring effects.

Beet Powder

Yes, this is made from ground-up beets, and it gives food a gorgeous ruby color and can be used in desserts as well as savory recipes to add nutritional value and a fun color. The powder form of beets is a great alternative if you're not a beet lover but still want to harvest the many nutrients beets offer.

Acai Powder

Acai powder is made from acai berries and can give your foods a subtle purple tint. They have been described as tasting like a cross between blackberries and unsweetened chocolate. And, yep, you guessed it, they are high in antioxidants and many nutrients too!

These powders aren't as "vibrant" as artificial food dyes, but for me, the benefits of adding these nutritious superfoods as opposed to adding toxic dyes to my diet made this a no-brainer.

GRAIN-FREE SUGAR COOKIES WITH MARBLE ICING

Up your sugar cookie game by dipping them in gorgeously swirled icing for a beautiful marble effect! These cookies look fancy, but I promise they are so simple to make.

Preheat the oven to 350°F (175°C). To make the flax eggs, combine the flaxseed meal and water in a small bowl and set it aside. In a separate bowl, whisk together the flour, salt and baking powder. In a separate bowl, whip the butter and sugar together in a stand mixer until creamy. Alternatively, you can use a hand beater. Once creamy, add the flax eggs and vanilla and almond extracts. You'll slowly add the flour mixture to the butter mixture, then add the milk until the cookie dough forms and sticks together.

To make rolling easier, divide the cookie dough in half. Place a sheet of parchment paper on the counter, set one half of the cookie dough on the paper, then set another sheet on top. Roll the dough out until it is roughly ¼ inch (6 mm) thick. Cut your cookies using a cookie cutter or glass into the desired shape. Repeat the process for the other half of the dough. Place the cookies on a parchment paper–lined baking sheet and bake for 10 minutes. You will likely need two baking sheets. Allow them to cool completely before icing.

To make the marble icing, whisk together the sugar and milk until you have a thick paste–like icing. I like to sift my confectioners' sugar to ensure there are no large clumps. Then, add a few drops of food coloring (preferably dye-free, natural food coloring) and, using a toothpick, spread it around to create a marble pattern, but don't mix it too much or you'll completely turn your icing one color. If you'd like to use superfood powders, you can either sprinkle the powders right into the icing and then use the toothpick to create the marble pattern, or you may also add a couple drops of water to each powder in a small bowl to make a liquid coloring, but don't add too much or it will dilute it and make your icing too watery. Carefully dip each cookie in the icing, top side down, and let the excess icing drip off. Place the cookies, un-iced side down, on a parchment paper–lined baking sheet or cooling rack to dry and allow the icing to harden. Add more coloring if desired and repeat until all the cookies are iced.

YIELD: *15–16 cookies*

SUGAR COOKIES

2 tbsp (14 g) flaxseed meal

5 tbsp (75 ml) water

3 cups (366 g) cassava flour

½ tsp salt

1 tbsp (14 g) baking powder

¾ cup (162 g) vegan butter

¾ cup (150 g) sugar (see Note)

1 tsp pure vanilla extract

½ tsp pure almond extract

3 tbsp (45 ml) plant milk

MARBLE ICING

1 cup (120 g) confectioners' sugar

2 tbsp (30 ml) plant milk

Plant-based food colorings or superfood powders such as pink pitaya, blue spirulina or matcha

---

NOTE: *You may substitute cane sugar with coconut sugar, but note the cookies may come out darker in color.*

OATMEAL MATCHA
ICE CREAM SANDWICHES

Matcha lovers, this one's for you! Matcha lattes may be all the rage, but what about matcha ice cream? That's right, you can add that powerhouse powder to your frozen treats too! I'm kicking it up a notch and stuffing this creamy matcha ice cream between two oatmeal cookies for the best summertime dessert.

You'll start by making the ice cream the day before. In a saucepan over medium heat, whisk together the solid coconut milk, vanilla, maple syrup, arrowroot powder and matcha powder until smooth and creamy. Pour the mixture into ice cube trays or a silicone mold and freeze overnight.

The next day, preheat the oven to 350°F (175°C). To make the cookies, in a large bowl, beat the butter until smooth, then add the sugar and beat until well combined. In a separate bowl, combine the flour, baking soda and salt, then slowly add it to the butter mixture, beating it until well combined. Turn your beater or mixer off, then stir in the milk and oats with a spatula or spoon. Roll ¼-cup (about 75-g) portions of batter with your hands into balls, then place them 2 inches (5 cm) apart on an ungreased baking sheet. Flatten each cookie with your hand and bake for 12 minutes. Remove them from the oven and let them cool completely.

While the cookies are cooling, blend the cubes of ice cream until you achieve a creamy ice cream texture, adding a splash of milk, if needed (but not too much!). Add a scoop of matcha ice cream to the bottom of one cookie and spread it almost to the edge, then top with another cookie. Repeat for the remaining cookies and ice cream.

YIELD: *4 ice cream sandwiches*

MATCHA ICE CREAM

1 (13.5-oz [400-ml]) can coconut milk, solid part only

2 tsp (10 ml) pure vanilla extract

⅓ cup (80 ml) pure maple syrup

1 tbsp (8 g) arrowroot powder

1 tsp matcha powder

OATMEAL COOKIES

½ cup (108 g) vegan butter, softened

¾ cup (98 g) coconut sugar

1¼ cups (185 g) gluten-free baking flour

½ tsp baking soda

¼ tsp salt

3 tbsp (45 ml) plant milk

1 cup (80 g) gluten-free quick oats

PITAYA
POACHED PEARS

Not only one of the easiest dessert recipes in this book, but also likely one of the prettiest—the pink pitaya powder does all of the work! Pitaya, also known as dragon fruit, is a gorgeous tropical fruit known for its high magnesium, fiber, iron, B2, vitamin C and antioxidant content. You can enjoy these poached pears as is or serve them with a dollop of coconut whipped cream or chocolate ganache.

Peel the pears, but leave the stems attached. In a large saucepan, whisk together the water, vanilla, agave or maple syrup, pink pitaya powder and salt and bring to a boil. Add the pears and boil for 15 to 20 minutes. Be sure to make sure the pears are fully submerged in the brine. If not, add a little more water until they are. Remove the saucepan from the heat and let the pears cool in the brine at room temperature, then place the saucepan in the refrigerator, letting the pears soak in the brine overnight. Serve with coconut whipped cream and chocolate ganache, if desired, but they are also great on their own.

NOTE: *The color of the pears will vary depending on how big the pears are, the brand of pitaya powder you use and how much water you use.*

YIELD: *5 servings*

5 small pears (Bosc pears work best)

½ gallon (2 L) water, enough to cover the pears

2 tsp (10 ml) pure vanilla extract

¼ cup (60 ml) agave or maple syrup

2 tbsp (24 g) pink pitaya powder

Pinch of salt

TOPPINGS (OPTIONAL)

Fluffy Coconut Whipped Cream (page 154)

Chocolate Ganache (page 158)

RASPBERRY JELL-O

Jell-O was always a favorite of mine growing up. My mom used to make Jell-O for me when I was sick, and it always helped me feel better. Unlike the boxed Jell-O mix though, we're making this raspberry Jell-O from scratch—real raspberries and all! But I promise it's so simple to make. I'm replacing the gelatin with agar agar powder to make this jiggly dessert vegan friendly and give it a boost of nutrients. The texture differs slightly from the Jell-O you might be used to, but this recipe is still a delicious plant-based substitute.

YIELD: *4–6 servings*

2½ cups (185 g) raspberries (may use frozen raspberries)

1½ cups (360 ml) water

⅓ cup (66 g) sugar or (80 ml) maple syrup

1 tsp agar agar powder

Fluffy Coconut Whipped Cream (page 154), for serving (optional)

In a saucepan over medium-high heat, add the raspberries and water and bring it to just below boiling. Let the raspberries reduce for about 10 minutes. Add the sugar or maple syrup and whisk to combine.

Pour the mixture into a blender and blend until smooth. Using a sieve or a fine-mesh strainer, strain the mixture back into the saucepan, discarding the seeds; the sieve should catch those. Place the saucepan back onto the burner and, on medium heat, bring the mixture back up to a simmer. Add the agar agar powder and whisk continuously for 3 to 5 minutes, until the mixture thickens.

Pour the mixture into ramekins, glasses or bowls and place them into the fridge to firm up, preferably overnight. Serve with a dollop of coconut whipped cream, if desired.

SALTED CINNAMON
HOT COCOA

Nothing beats a cozy cup of hot cocoa in the wintertime. This dairy-free hot cocoa features the antioxidant-rich, rawest form of cocoa: cacao powder, blended with cinnamon and a hint of salt for the most deliciously silky, warming treat. This hot cocoa is ready in a matter of minutes and is also naturally sweetened.

Heat the milk in a saucepan over medium-high heat. Whisk in the cacao powder, cinnamon, salt, vanilla and maple syrup. Bring the mixture to a boil, whisking frequently, then remove from the heat. Serve with a dollop of coconut whipped cream and raw cacao nibs, if desired.

NOTE: *Double the recipe to enjoy with a loved one!*

YIELD: *1–2 servings*

HOT COCOA
1½ cups (360 ml) plant milk
2 tbsp (11 g) raw cacao powder
½ tsp cinnamon
Pinch of salt
½ tsp pure vanilla extract
2 tbsp (30 ml) maple syrup

TOPPINGS (OPTIONAL)
Fluffy Coconut Whipped Cream (page 154)
Cacao nibs

DEATH BY CHOCOLATE
MUG CAKE

Skip the fuss and the oven with this Death by Chocolate Mug Cake recipe! It's moist, delicious and perfect for serving one or two people, and it's unarguably the quickest and easiest dessert recipe in this book. It's the I-want-chocolate-cake-and-I-want-it-now dessert, ready in just two minutes. I highly recommend enjoying this chocolate cake with a scoop of my homemade No-Churn Vanilla & Chocolate Ice Cream (page 153) for extra deliciousness!

In a mug, add the flour, sugar, cocoa powder, baking powder and salt and stir gently with a fork to combine. Then add the nut or seed butter, vanilla and coconut cream, and gently stir until a batter forms.

Microwave on high for 45 to 55 seconds, garnish with chocolate chips, if desired, then let it cool for a minute or two before enjoying. Top with store-bought vegan ice cream or my No-Churn Vanilla & Chocolate Ice Cream, if desired.

YIELD: *1 mug cake*

2 tbsp (15 g) banana flour

2 tbsp (16 g) coconut sugar

2 tbsp (11 g) unsweetened cocoa powder

¼ tsp baking powder

Pinch of salt

3 tbsp (48 g) nut or seed butter

½ tsp pure vanilla extract

3 tbsp (45 ml) coconut cream (or other plant milk)

Dark chocolate chips, for garnishing (optional)

No-Churn Vanilla & Chocolate Ice Cream (page 153), for serving (optional)

Dessert Swap
STAPLES

As I began working on this book, "Dessert Swap Staples" wasn't originally a chapter I was going to include. But as I was developing the other recipes in later chapters, I found myself using a lot of these swaps either in the recipes or as a topping, so I thought it would be super helpful to have a section including my most common go-to recipes to either enhance your gluten-free vegan dessert experience or even just to indulge in on their own.

So, what are some of the most common recipes people are looking to adapt to be gluten-free and/or vegan?

Pie Crust
Of course, gluten-free pie crust is a popular search, but I'm giving you a special, family gluten-free *and* vegan pie crust recipe that is so flaky and tender, you'd never know the difference. The thing that I find differs the most when making gluten-free vegan pie crust is the inability to roll it and mold it seamlessly in your pie plate in one big sheet. Although it is doable, gluten-free dough isn't as stretchy and elastic as traditional pie crust—that is gluten's job after all. But don't worry, there's a work-around to ensure your pie crust looks and tastes fabulous! I like to press the dough into the sides of the pie/tart pan first and then press the dough into the bottom. It bakes nicely that way and also allows for a deeper well to fill it with your favorite filling.

Frosting
Delicious buttercream frosting that's good on any cake or cookie or even stuffed in between two cookies to make the most scrumptious cookie sammies is a must! My buttercream is simply made with just three ingredients, and my favorite flavor addition is a pinch of cinnamon to make it extra delicious. Sometimes I will use vegan shortening in my frosting for a bit of a lighter texture, and when I do, I will note that in the recipe.

Ice Cream

You scream, I scream . . . we all scream for (vegan) ice cream! Making your own ice cream at home isn't anything new, but making your own *vegan* ice cream at home may be new to you, at least the way I make it. Why? Well, first of all, there is no fancy ice cream machine needed to make the most creamy and delicious vegan ice cream at home. So don't worry, you don't need to buy another appliance to enjoy delicious, no-churn ice cream. You simply heat the ice cream base—I like to use coconut milk for extra creaminess, but you can also use oat milk or cashew milk too. Then freeze it in ice cube trays or silicone molds overnight and blend it in your blender until it's smooth and creamy then serve! Too good to be true? Nope! You can certainly experiment with other flavors, but head to my vanilla and chocolate ice cream recipe (page 153) for the most classic swap or accompaniment with your favorite desserts.

Whipped Cream

Ditch the Cool Whip© and make your own at home in less than 15 minutes! This whipped cream is made with coconut milk, so if you're not a coconut fan, you'll probably want to skip this one, but I happen to find this coconut whipped cream especially delicious on my pumpkin pie. I also like that I have complete control over how much sugar goes into my whipped cream when I'm watching my sugar intake.

Caramel

Did you ever think there would come a day where you would make vegan caramel? Let me tell you, this caramel is magical. I put it on and in everything, eat it with a spoon and even make fudge out of it! You can make this caramel nut-free too if you're avoiding nuts. The one caveat is you have to pay very close attention to the order you put the ingredients together in, as well as giving it your full attention while whisking almost constantly. But don't fret, it only takes a few minutes to make this silky golden perfection.

Chocolate Ganache

Chocolate ganache is probably the easiest swap to make, and it provides that added oomph to your desserts. I like to use oat milk in place of the traditional heavy cream to make my chocolate ganache, but you could also try cashew milk or any other plant milk. I would suggest staying away from using full-fat coconut milk though, as it makes the ganache too solid when it cools. Try topping your cakes, brownies, bars and even cookies with chocolate ganache for that extra yum factor!

SIMPLE BUTTERCREAM FROSTING

Making buttercream frosting is back on the table! With the amazing vegan butter substitutes readily available at most grocery stores now, you can still enjoy a creamy, fluffy buttercream frosting that is so simple to whip up.

In a stand mixer (alternatively, you can do this with a hand blender or mixer), cream the butter, cinnamon and vanilla on medium speed. Slowly add in the sugar and keep blending until it thickens.

NOTE: *For a lighter buttercream frosting, use ½ cup (108 g) of vegan butter and ½ cup (103 g) of vegan shortening.*

YIELD: *2 cups (480 ml)*

1 cup (215 g) vegan butter
¼ tsp cinnamon
1 tsp pure vanilla extract
4 cups (480 g) confectioners' sugar

LIGHT & FLAKY
PIE CRUST

This tender and flaky pie crust recipe was handed down from my grandmother to my dad and now to me. It has always been my favorite pie crust, and luckily converting it to a gluten-free vegan version is, well, easy as pie!

Grease a 9-inch (23-cm) pie plate. In a large bowl, whisk together the flours, sugar (if using) and salt. Add both the oil and butter and knead the dough with your hands or a pastry cutter. Add the water and continue to knead until your pie dough can roll into a ball. Press the dough into the sides of your pie plate first, then press the rest of the dough into the bottom of the pie plate.

To blind-bake the crust, preheat the oven to 350°F (175°C) and use a fork to prick the bottom of the crust in several places. Depending on what recipe you're making, you can pre-bake the crust for about 10 minutes. If the recipe calls for a longer baking time, it's not necessary to pre-bake the crust.

NOTES: *This also works if making a tart shell or for savory recipes! For a grain-free crust, simply swap out the gluten-free baking flour 1:1 with cassava flour!*

YIELD: *1 (9-inch [23-cm]) pie crust*

2 cups (296 g) gluten-free baking flour

½ cup (56 g) coconut flour

2 tbsp (16 g) coconut or date sugar (optional)

1 tsp salt

⅓ cup (80 g) coconut oil, softened but not completely melted

½ cup (108 g) vegan butter

6 to 7 tbsp (90 to 105 ml) water, ice cold

NO-CHURN VANILLA & CHOCOLATE ICE CREAM

Have you made your own ice cream at home before? It's a lot easier than you think, and there's no fancy ice cream maker needed to make these simple coconut milk–based ice creams! You simply heat, freeze, blend and serve!

In a saucepan over medium heat, whisk together the solid coconut milk, vanilla, maple syrup, arrowroot powder and cocoa powder (if using) until smooth and creamy. Pour the mixture into ice cube trays and freeze overnight. The next day, blend the cubes of ice cream until you achieve a creamy ice cream texture, adding a splash of milk if needed (but not too much!). Enjoy immediately and place the remaining ice cream in an airtight container and store in the freezer.

NOTE: *After freezing the leftover ice cream, allow it to sit out for about 5 minutes to soften just a bit before enjoying.*

YIELD: *4 servings*

1 (13.5-oz [400-ml]) can coconut milk, solid part only

2 tsp (10 ml) pure vanilla extract

⅓ cup (80 ml) pure maple syrup

1 tbsp (8 g) arrowroot powder

2 tbsp (11 g) unsweetened cocoa powder (optional)

FLUFFY COCONUT
WHIPPED CREAM

Making your own dairy-free whipped cream at home is so simple using full-fat coconut milk. I also like to make my own because it seems to be extra fluffy compared to store-bought, and I can control just how sweet it is. This whipped cream is made with only three ingredients and will keep in your fridge for up to one week, so it's easy to make ahead of time for the holidays and maybe keep on hand anytime for when a dollop of whipped cream makes the perfect finishing touch on your next dessert.

Roughly 10 to 15 minutes before making the whipped cream, place your mixing bowl in the fridge or freezer to chill. Scoop out the solid coconut cream from the coconut milk can and place it into the chilled mixing bowl. You will want to discard the coconut water on the bottom of the can or save it to use in another recipe; it makes a great addition to smoothies!

Using a hand beater, beat the coconut cream for about 1 minute until it starts to become fluffy, then add the vanilla and sweetener and mix for a couple more minutes until it's smooth and creamy. The whipped cream is ready to enjoy right away or you can store it in the fridge for up to 1 week in a sealed container.

NOTES: *How firm or soft the coconut milk is may determine which sweetener you should use. If the coconut cream is too soft, you may want to use cane or confectioners' sugar instead of a liquid sweetener.*

I always like to keep a can of coconut milk in my fridge at all times just in case I need it. It also helps to chill a large mixing bowl in the freezer to keep the whipped cream from melting while you whip it up.

YIELD: *4 servings*

1 (13.5-oz [400-ml]) can coconut milk, solid part only, chilled in the fridge overnight

1 to 2 tsp (5 to 10 ml) pure vanilla extract

1 to 2 tbsp (15 to 30 ml) agave syrup or other sweetener of choice (maple syrup, cane sugar or confectioners' sugar)

VEGAN
CARAMEL SAUCE

Say hello to your new favorite filling, dip, spread and eat-from-the-jar sweet treat! It only takes a few minutes to make your own vegan caramel on your stovetop using seven simple ingredients. Here are some ideas on how to use it: brownies, waffles, pancakes, toast, muffins, cake, cookies, cupcakes or with fresh fruit! You can even chill it in a candy mold for a pop-in-your-mouth caramel fudge goodie. I like to use sunflower seed butter, which also makes this caramel nut free!

In a small saucepan, melt the butter or oil over high heat. Once melted, whisk in the maple syrup. Then, whisk in the solid coconut cream. Whisking continuously, add the sunflower seed butter and continue to whisk until the mixture starts to thicken. Turn the heat to low and whisk in the vanilla, salt and baking soda (if using) and keep whisking until the sauce is smooth.

NOTE: *Any nut or seed butter will work; the flavor just might vary slightly.*

YIELD: *about ½ cup (120 ml)*

3 tbsp (42 g) vegan butter (may substitute with coconut oil instead if you wish)

2 tbsp (30 ml) maple syrup

2 tbsp (30 g) coconut milk, solid part only

2 tbsp (32 g) sunflower seed butter

¼ tsp pure vanilla extract

Pinch of salt

½ tsp baking soda, for a more caramel color (optional)

CHOCOLATE GANACHE

With the potential to add the wow factor to any dessert you please, and the ease with which it's made, this chocolate topping is bound to be a book favorite! I especially love to add this on top of my Baked Chocolate Ganache Cheesecake (page 37) for the ultimate chocolate lover's delight.

In a medium saucepan, heat the milk over medium-high heat until it starts to slowly boil. Add the chocolate chips, salt and maple syrup (if using), and stir it with a whisk until the chocolate chips start to melt. Remove from the heat and continue to whisk until the ganache is smooth and creamy. The ganache will thicken as it cools, but if you're using it as a topping and want to have a drizzle effect, pour the ganache over your dessert when it's cool but still pourable. Keep it stored in an airtight container on your counter for up to 3 days.

YIELD: *2 cups (480 ml)*

1¼ cups (300 ml) oat milk (or other plant milk, but do not use full-fat coconut milk)

1⅓ cups (223 g) dark chocolate chips

Pinch of salt

1 to 2 tbsp (15 to 30 ml) maple syrup (optional)

SPECIAL INGREDIENTS & FAVORITE BRANDS

Bob's Red Mill® Gluten-Free 1:1 Baking Flour

Bob's Red Mill® Cassava Flour

Bob's Red Mill® Almond Flour

Edward & Sons Trading Company, Inc.® Banana Flour

Edward & Sons Trading Company, Inc.® Cassava Flour

Edward & Sons Trading Company, Inc.® Sweet Potato Flour

Califia Farms® Plant-Based Milks

Elmhurst 1925® Plant-Based Milks

Oatsome™ Organic Oat Milk

Melt Organic™ Plant Butter

Miyoko's Creamery Organic Vegan Butter

Kite Hill® Vegan Cream Cheese

Kite Hill® Plant-Based Yogurt

Nutiva® Coconut Sugar

Nutiva® Cacao Powder

Nutiva® Shortening

Hu® Dark Chocolate Chunks

Enjoy Life Foods® Dark Chocolate Chips & Mini Chips

Lily's® Chocolate Chips

Lakanto® Monk Fruit Sweetened Chocolate Chips

Nairn's Gluten-Free Oat Grahams

WHERE TO BUY SPECIAL INGREDIENTS

Sometimes I use ingredients in my recipes that are unique, and they might be ones you've never heard of before. While stores vary depending on where you live, you can find a lot of these items at natural foods stores, like Whole Foods, Trader Joe's, Sprouts, Natural Grocers, Fresh Thyme or even at Kroger, Meijer, etc. I also find a lot of items on Amazon (my go-to!). You can even google items and find them online, like from Thrive Market, Bob's Red Mill, Edward & Sons Trading Company, Inc., Nutiva and Suncore Foods®, to name a few. Natural products are becoming more widespread, which is really great, but they are also starting to include them into the same sections as opposed to having their own sections at the grocery stores, so keep your eyes peeled for those alternatives and take a few extra minutes to read nutrition/ingredient labels.

Health Coaching Tip: The fewer ingredients an item has, usually the better. Also, make sure sugar isn't in the first three ingredients listed. Items with sugar listed lower in the list of ingredients will have a lower sugar content.

ACKNOWLEDGMENTS

First and foremost, I want to thank God for allowing me to do this work to help people, to hopefully be a light and for graciously showing me a better way. Seven years ago, I fasted and prayed for better health and relief from my ailments and He delivered in such a huge, unexpected way. Lord, may you also do the same for others in this way as you have done for me. God, I hope you are glorified in the work I am doing and with the heart in which I serve.

"So whether you eat or drink or whatever you do, do it all for the glory of God."
—1 Cor 10:31

To my husband, Ben, your willingness to change your diet right along with the need to change mine has been one of the most supportive ways you've shown your love for me. It has fueled me to keep going and continue this important work. Thank you so much! Oh, and thanks for being my hand model and dishwasher too!

To my son, Read, and my daughter, Eliana, you're too young now, but when you read this in years to come, I want you to know just how loved you are and how much I value serving you healthy, whole foods that help your little bodies develop to help you be the best you can be. I enjoy baking with you so very much, and I hope it is something you carry with you. Thank you for being my little bakers and taste testers. I hope that one day we can run Healthy Little Vittles together!

Dad, thanks for being my number one taste tester! In all seriousness, I appreciate and am grateful for your baking wisdom to help me really nail these recipes and allowing me to share some of our modified family recipes with the world!

To the rest of my family and friends, thank you so much for your support. I know you probably questioned our lifestyle a lot as we started on this journey, and who knew it would lead me to write this book! But you believed in me and you all have really put forth such an effort to cook "safe" meals for me to eat around the holidays, and I'm truly grateful for your thoughtfulness.

Thank you, Marissa, for guiding me in my work on this book and for giving me the opportunity to bring my sweet passion to life. Thank you, Laura, Meg and the rest of the Page Street team for helping me with the images and the design of this book and for granting me this opportunity to reach more people, to help more people and to hopefully be a light to people who might be feeling hopeless when it comes to such a huge part of our culture—enjoying delicious desserts!

(continued)

Thank you, Beata Lubas, for your constant food photography inspiration; you are truly one of the most talented food photographers in the business, and I'm so grateful for your book *How to Photograph Food*. Your book helped me immensely for this project to take my food photography to the next level.

Thank you, Natalie Thomas from Feasting on Fruit, for always wanting to collaborate with me and for being such a great friend. Thank you for inspiring a couple of these recipes, ones that we originally worked on together. You show such kindness and are a true example of community over competition.

Thank you so much, Susan from Sweetheart Ceramics, for your amazing talent in creating your ceramicware, many used in this book! They really elevate my photos; I love your work so much!

Finally, a heartfelt thank-you to all my Healthy Little Vittles followers. I would not be where I am without you. You help hold *me* accountable when times are hard to stick with it and keep fueling forward. To other bloggers who have inspired me, helped me grow and shared my content (even when it wasn't even related to your own), thank you from the bottom of my heart. Keep spreading love and kindness!

ABOUT THE AUTHOR

Based in Columbus, Ohio, Gina Fontana is the recipe developer, food photographer, certified health coach and personality behind Healthy Little Vittles, a popular health food blog focusing on gluten-free, vegan and plant-based recipes. In 2013, after a lifelong search for answers to her unexplained health ailments, Gina was diagnosed with thyroid disease. Switching to a gluten-free, plant-based diet transformed her life, prompting Gina to share her journey with others. Through her story, recipes and creative photography, Gina's mission is to inspire people to pursue a healthier lifestyle and to enjoy all of life's moments without giving up on indulgent foods, but rather finding a different way of making them, like many of the recipes in this book.

Gina's first published 55-recipe book titled *Moon Milk* is being sold worldwide! She has also been featured on the cover of *Simply Gluten Free* magazine, in the pages of *Elle* magazine, on BuzzFeed and on Lauren Conrad's blog. Currently, she lives with her husband, four-year-old son, two-year-old daughter and two fur babies in a quaint neighborhood and enjoys working from home. When she's not cooking in the kitchen, mom-ing or working on her blog, she enjoys going to church, singing, exercising, playing softball, learning piano, going for walks and watching her favorite TV shows.

LET'S CONNECT!

I am so excited you've found me somehow in the vast world we live in. I have to believe you were led to me for a reason, and I am so glad to welcome you to the Vittle Club. I am so very humbled that I get to do this work and hopefully initiate changes in the lives of those needing it most. My blog, Healthy Little Vittles, has been a labor of love, one that I cherish and pray continues to grow. Social media alone has allowed me to connect with so many wonderful people all over the world, and now through this book I'll connect with many more. I couldn't be more grateful! I truly value the friendships that I've made and cherish being part of a community of like-minded individuals. Speaking of social media, go ahead and find me on Instagram @HealthyLittleVittles to stay up to date with all my new culinary creations, both sweet and savory, giving you ideas of how you can stick with this lifestyle change right alongside me. I am still making changes every day.

If you make any of these dessert recipes, feel free to tag me on Instagram or use #HealthyLittleSweets so I can see all your lovely re-creations and what you're all loving the most! And feel free to reach out with any questions/feedback you may have any time.

Many sweet, healthy blessings to you, my friends!

INDEX

THE BEGINNER'S GUIDE TO *Gluten-Free* VEGAN BAKING

PAGE STREET
PUBLISHING CO.

First published in 2021 by
Page Street Publishing Co.
27 Congress Street, Suite 105
Salem, MA 01970
www.pagestreetpublishing.com

Distributed by Macmillan, sales in Canada by The Canadian Manda Group.

25   24   23   22   21   1   2   3   4   5

ISBN-13: 978-1-64567-430-6
ISBN-10: 1-64567-430-4

Library of Congress Control Number: 2021931950

Cover and book design by Meg Baskis for Page Street Publishing Co.
Photography by Gina Fontana; author photo on page 163 by Meghan McGuire

Printed and bound in the United States